Fundamentals of
Decoding for Teachers

Fundamentals of Decoding for Teachers

Leo M. Schell

Kansas State University

RAND McNALLY COLLEGE PUBLISHING COMPANY / Chicago

Current printing   (last digit)
15   14   13   12   11   10   9   8   7   6

Dedicated with pleasure
to Paul C. Burns

Table of Contents

Introduction

This is an ordinary book in which the material is presented in a non-ordinary fashion. The contents deal with information about decoding—phonemic and morphemic analysis—which has been found to be of value to prospective elementary school teachers and those teachers currently involved in reading instruction.

The basic concept behind the manner of presentation of material in this book is that you, the reader, are expected to do <u>something</u> other than just read as you progress through this book. That "something" happens to be answering questions and making decisions.

You will be strongly tempted NOT to write or mark the answers but only to say or look at them. FOR BEST LEARNING, IT IS STRONGLY RECOMMENDED THAT YOU CONSISTENTLY RESPOND IN WRITING <u>BEFORE</u> LOOKING AT THE ANSWERS!

Since you will give answers to questions, you need to know whether you have answered correctly. This is where the arrangement of the material in this book will assist you. The following is an example of the techniques used to present the contents.

Each page is divided into two parts, a right-hand column and a left-hand column. Information, questions, and exercises are presented in the right-hand column. Answers are presented in the other column, the one on the l___-hand side of the page.

It is hoped that you automatically read the word "left" when you saw "l___." If so, then you have already caught on to the system in which much of the material in this book is presented.

However, this is only one-half of the system. To let you know immediately whether you made the correct answer, the answers will be left   presented in the l____-hand column as shown here. Because we don't want you to see the answers until you have read and answered the questions, a "mask" is provided. (The "mask" can be created by removing a portion of the back cover at the perforation.) Each time you have completed your response, move the "mask" down and the answer will appear in the left-hand column opposite your response.

Last, you will be asked to pronounce and listen to many words and to match them with other words containing the same sound. Usually you will agree with the book's answers; infrequently you may not. The primary reason you may disagree is the dialect influence found within the various areas of our country. A student in Maine probably says and hears words slightly differently from one in New Jersey who in turn probably says and hears the same words slightly differently from one in South Carolina. Etc., ad infinitum.

Pre-Assessment

As an elementary school teacher, YOU know far more about mathematics, spelling, grammar, etc. than you will ever have to teach elementary school pupils. But how much do you know about the content of decoding that you will be required to teach these children? Let's find out! Check the correct answer in each example.

1. A syllable is
    _____A. two or more letters with one sound.
    _____B. the smallest possible speech sound.
C   _____C. a speech unit with one vowel sound.

2. In which "word" does the underlined letter represent a "short vowel" sound?
C   _____A. splight   _____B. men' sor   _____C. plidge

3. Which is the phonetic symbol for the schwa sound?

A   _____A. ə   _____B. ô   _____C. ă

4. In which word does the underlined letters represent a vowel diphthong?

C   _____A. r<u>ou</u>gh   B. sl<u>ow</u>   _____C. <u>oy</u>ster

5. How many phonemes in *marriage?*

D   _____A. 2   _____B. 3   _____C. 4   _____D. 5

6. Which word contains a consonant digraph?

A   _____A. bushel   _____B. sign   _____C. daughter

7. Which word contains the unvoiced *th* sound?

B   _____A. <u>th</u>ere   _____B. <u>th</u>orn   _____C. <u>th</u>em

8. Which is the correct syllabication for "budable"?

B   _____A. bu′ da ble   _____B. bud′ a ble   _____C. bu′ dab le

9. In which "word" does the underlined letter represent a glided vowel sound?

A   _____A. bl<u>a</u>′ fut   _____B. spl<u>a</u>re   _____C. cr<u>a</u>ll

10. Which "word" is syllabicated and accented wrongly?

        _____A. lop′ i cap ping   _____B. let ha′ ble

B   _____C. am bil′ i ty

Number possible-10   Number wrong-_____   Number right-_____

SELF-EVALUATION

_____I need to study this book carefully since I know only some of its contents.

_____I had better work feverishly since I know almost nothing about phonics!

Vowels and Consonants

Remember?

    Teacher: "The vowels are *a, e, i, o, u* and sometimes *w* and *y*. What are the other letters called?"

    Children: "Consonants."

Remember? Of course you do!

But what differentiates a vowel from a consonant, what makes an *a* different from a *b*?

Carefully pronounce the sound *a* represents in *add;* now just the sound *e* represents in *elk;* last, just the sound *i* represents in *imp.*

Pronounce them once again. Pay particular attention to the movement of your tongue and lips. The letters that you just pronounced all represent [vowel sounds, consonant sounds].

vowel sounds

Now try to pronounce only the sound *t* represents in *toe,* only *f* in *fee* and *j* in *jet.* Again pay close attention to the movement of your tongue and lips. The letters that you just pronounced all represent [vowel sounds, consonant sounds].

consonant sounds

It should be obvious that the lips and tongue move *less* in pronouncing a vowel sound than they do when pronouncing a [vowel sound, consonant sound].

consonant sound

To produce a consonant sound, the tongue and lips move [more, less] than they do to pronounce a vowel sound.

more

In producing a consonant sound, the breath channel is *blocked* and *narrowed* at some particular point. Usually the tongue and/or lips are responsible for the _____ .

blocking, or narrowing

If consonant sounds and vowel sounds differ, then we must conclude that in producing a vowel sound, the breath channel is NOT _____ or narrowed.

blocked

We have talked so far about "breath channel," "blocking," and "pronunciation" and we have almost completely ignored the letters *a*, *e*, *i*, *o*, and *u*. We have been more interested in speech *sounds* than in alphabetical *letters.* This is because linguists define consonants and vowels primarily as speech [sounds, letters] rather than as alphabetical [sounds, letters].

sounds

letters

It should be apparent by now that your elementary school teacher was wrong! The letters *a*, *e*, *i*, *o*, and *u* [are, are not] vowels. Rather they are [sounds, letters] that represent various speech [sounds, letters]. The letters *b*, *c*, *d*, etc. are not consonants. Rather they are [sounds, letters] that represent various speech [sounds, letters]. A vowel is really a speech sound—and so is a consonant!

In this book, to avoid confusion, we will try to use phrases such as "vowel letters" and "consonant letters" and "vowel sounds" and "consonant sounds."

Phonemes and Graphemes

There are 26 letters in our alphabet. But, for all practical purposes, there are 19 more sounds than there are letters. Thus, there are [44, 45, 46] sounds in our language.* But linguists prefer—and educators have adopted—the term *phoneme* rather than the word *sound*.

The only difference between the pronunciation of the words *bit* and *pit* is the initial sounds or phon____ represented by the consonant letters *b* and *p*.

Similarly, the only difference between the pronunciation of *pig* and *peg* is the vowel sounds or [phonemes, letters] represented by the vowel letters *i* and *e*.

Spoken words are composed of a series of connected sounds or [letters, phonemes]. In the spoken word *cat*, how many individual phonemes are rapidly blended together? 1 2 3

Pronounce each word below; write the number of phonemes you hear in each. DON'T GET FOOLED!

is   _____ phonemes

red   _____ phonemes

left margin answers:
are not
letters; sounds
letters; sounds

45

emes

phonemes

phonemes
3

2
3

---

*Various linguists do not agree on the number of sounds in our language. Each professes a specific amount—38 to 47—depending on the dialectal variations each considers significant. For the purpose of this book, the total of 45 sounds will be used.

4	baby	_____phonemes	
4	dream	_____phonemes	
5	daughter	_____phonemes	

Four phonemes in *dream* and only five in *daughter?* How come? In *is* there are two phonemes and two letters; in *red,* three of each, and in *baby,* four of each. Why not eight in *daughter?*

The reason is that even though *in general* American-English spelling follows a system of one-to-one correspondence between sound and letter, this relationship is far from perfect. In many words one letter represents one phoneme. But when there are 19 more phonemes than there are letters (or graphemes) to represent them, absolute one-to-one correspondence is impossible.

In dictionaries, each word has two entries, a spelling entry and a pronunciation entry. Here are spelling and pronunciation entries for the words you pronounced on pages 5 and 6. Write the number of phonemes in each word and the number of symbols in each pronunciation entry.

	Spelling Entry	Pronunciation Entry	Phonemes	Pronunciation Symbols
2; 2	is	iz	_____	_____
3; 3	red	red	_____	_____
4; 4	ba by	bā′ bē	_____	_____
4; 4	dream	drēm	_____	_____
5; 5	daugh ter	dô′ tər	_____	_____

Thus, each symbol in a pronunciation entry of a dictionary is a written

phoneme

representation of one sound, or one _____, in the spoken word.

But it is obvious that in written English, each of the 45 phonemes

cannot; letter

[can, cannot] be represented by one and only one _____ of the alphabet. Sometimes, as in *dream* (drēm) and *daughter* (dô′ tər), more

sound or phoneme

than one letter is used to represent one _____.

And just as linguists use the specific word *phoneme* rather than the general word *sound,* so they also have a special name for the written symbols *in our spelling system* that represent phonemes. These are called *graphemes*. As each of the various phoneme-grapheme correspondences is presented in this book, you will be introduced to the phonemic symbols used by linguists. To aid your understanding of these phonemic symbols, the graphemes that represent these symbols are included as are the dictionary pronunciation symbols. Since the phonemic symbols represent spoken sounds, the symbols are enclosed in slashes: /a/, /ey/, /ow/.

In the written word *baby*, the final phoneme, /iy/ or "long *e* sound," is represented by the grapheme [e, y]. In *dream,* the vowel phoneme (again "long *e*") is represented by the grapheme _____ which is composed of the two letters *e* and *a*. And in *daughter* the first vowel phoneme, /ɔ/ or circumflex *o*, is represented by the grapheme _____.

y

ea

au

Most often in English spelling, each phoneme is represented by a single letter grapheme as in *up* and *consist*. But frequently, as in *road* (rōd) and phonics (fŏn′ iks), a phoneme is represented by a grapheme composed of [1, 2] letters. And occasionally, one phoneme is represented by a grapheme composed of three letters as in *watch* where the *tch* represents one phoneme, /č/.

2

This lack of one-to-one correspondence between spelling and pronunciation is most obvious and frequent with regard to vowel phonemes and graphemes but it also holds true for certain consonant phonemes and graphemes as we shall see later.

ON YOUR OWN! Look up the dictionary pronunciation entry of each of these words. Write it and the number of phonemes in the word. The first one is done for you.

Answers to dictionary pronunciation entries are not given since different dictionaries use different symbols.

Word	Pronunciation Entry	Phonemes
free	frē	3
said	_____	_____
phase	_____	_____
marriage	_____	_____
naughty	_____	_____

Review #1

1. The vowel sounds are *a*, *e*, *i*, *o*, *u* and sometimes *w* and *y*.   True

False   False

consonant sound

vowel sound

sound

sound

phoneme

2. The breath channel is blocked or narrowed more while producing a [consonant sound, vowel sound] than while producing a [consonant sound, vowel sound].

3. To a linguist, a vowel is really a [sound, letter].

4. To a linguist, a consonant is really a [sound, letter].

5. The smallest unit of sound in a word is called a _____.

6. Pronounce each word; how many phonemes in each one?

3	bought	_____	phonemes
3	league	_____	phonemes
5	announce	_____	phonemes

phoneme

7. Each symbol in a pronunciation entry in a dictionary represents a single [phoneme, grapheme].

grapheme

8. A letter or group of letters representing a phoneme is called a _____.

False

9. In our spelling system, words contain an equal number of letters and graphemes.   True   False

True

10. A vowel phoneme may be represented by a grapheme of one letter as in *wall* or by more than one letter as in *rough*.   True   False

True

11. A consonant phoneme may be represented by a grapheme of one letter or by more than one letter.   True   False

SELF-EVALUATION #1

Of 11 items, I correctly answered _____. I feel this is:

_____Excellent   _____Fair   _____Yechhhh!

Vowel Phonemes

Vowel Phonemes: I

āviary   īcon   ūsurp   ōnus   ēgress

Examination of the above words should lead you to conclude that all of them have something in common. The diacritical markings above the initial *vowel* letters are all [alike, different].

alike

This symbol is called a macron (mā′ krŏn or măk′ rən). It indicates that the sound represented by the marked vowel letter is the same as the name of that vowel letter in the alphabet. We tell elementary school pupils that such a vowel letter "says its own [name, sound]."

name

Usually we tell children that these phonemes are called "long vowel sounds." But some linguists feel this term is inaccurate; they prefer the term *glided* vowel sounds. The reason they prefer glided is because the tongue usually rises as these sounds are being produced and the sounds "glide" from one place in the mouth to another. (If you say these sounds slowly and separately, you can feel your tongue move slightly.)

Complete this equation:

glided

ā, ē, ī, ō, ū = long vowel sounds = _____ vowel phonemes.

Linguists use the following phonemic symbols to represent the glided vowel phonemes.

ā = /ey/   ē = /iy/   ī = /ay/   ō = /ow/   ū = /yuw/

TEST YOURSELF! Check each word that contains a glided vowel phoneme and put a macron above the vowel letter representing this sound.

concrēte; wāive

_____concrete   _____urgent   _____waive

mōtel

_____motel   _____tower   _____mimic

Vowel Phonemes: II

ădjunct   ŏmnibus

ĕmpirical   ŭlterior

ĭntrepid   ĕccentric

vowel

Each word above begins with a [vowel, consonant] letter and a vowel sound.

identical

And each of these initial vowel letters is marked with [identical, different] diacritical markings. This diacritical mark is called a *breve* (brēv or brĕv). (Some dictionaries do not use any diacritical mark at all for this phoneme but merely the pronunciation symbol *a, e, i, o,* or *u*.)

breve

A [breve, macron] is used to mark the common vowel phonemes called the "short" or unglided vowel sound.

Linguists use the following phonemic symbols to represent the unglided vowel phonemes.

ă = /æ/   ĕ = /e/   ĭ = /i/   ŏ = /a/   ŭ = /ə/

For each phoneme you learn in this book, you should have a key word, a word you can easily associate with it. Here are some possible

short

ones for unglided, or _____, vowel phonemes.

A̲tlantic   e̲bony   I̲ndian   o̲bsolete   u̲ltimate

a̲valanche   e̲ducator   i̲nsect   O̲ctober   u̲mpire

Pronounce each word *naturally*. Check the ones containing a short or unglided vowel sound and put a breve above the vowel letter representing this sound. (Hint: Can a word contain two short vowel sounds?)

clĭp; mŏnotone; jŭnction

_____ clip   _____ monotone   _____ junction

grămmar

_____ grammar   _____ create   _____ disease

bŏmbăstĭc; wrĕstle*

_____ bombastic   _____ viceroy   _____ wrestle

---

*Not everyone reading these words will pronounce them with a unglided phoneme. If you didn't, don't worry. These are *dictionary* pronunciations, not necessarily *your* pronunciations.

Vowel Phonemes: III

Check each word that does NOT contain either a glided or an unglided vowel phoneme.

arm; for   _____arm   _____phone   _____for

sir; burn   _____sun   _____sir   _____burn

care   _____care   _____add   _____road

Pronounce carefully each word you checked. How many different vowel phonemes can you hear *all together* in these five words?

4   1   2   3   4   5

r   Write the letter that immediately follows the vowel letter in each of these words. _____

The phoneme /r/ affects our pronunciation of almost all of the vowel phonemes that precede it in a syllable. Thus, we call one group of vowel

r   phonemes "_____-controlled" sounds.

The most frequently used children's dictionaries list only four different r-controlled sounds—but not all of them use the same pronunciation symbols to represent these sounds.

Pronunciation Symbols	Phoneme	As In	Key Phrase
âr; ãr	/ær/	care, pair, wear	Rare bear chair
är	/ər/	car	Far star
ûr, ėr	/ar/	were, blur, sir	Stir her fur
ôr	/ɔr/	corn	Worn horn

Write *ar* if a word contains the /ər/ phoneme (car); *ur* if the /ar/ phoneme (were, fur); and *or* if the /ɔr/ phoneme (corn).

ur; ar; ur   _____learn   _____sergeant   _____worm

or; or; ar   _____reward   _____hoarse   _____guard

Vowel Phonemes: IV

Check the three words that do NOT contain a glided, unglided, nor r-controlled vowel phoneme.

stall

_____ stall	_____ mercy	_____ cave
_____ barn	_____ test	_____ stock
_____ grow	_____ bought	_____ straw

bought; straw

This phoneme is known as the circumflex *o*. It is represented by the pronunciation symbol ô and by the phonemic symbol $/ɔ/$.*

Check the following words in which this vowel phoneme occurs. Listen for the sound—don't be fooled by letters or spelling patterns!

thaw; pause

_____ thaw	_____ pause	_____ shall
_____ talk	_____ mallet	_____ crawl
_____ author	_____ malt	_____ sought

talk; crawl

author; malt; sought

One possible set of key words to help you remember this circumflex *o* (ô) phoneme might be: *tall daughter.*

Write one or more memorable key word phrases to help you remember this phoneme.

_____   _____

Vowel Phonemes: V

Pronounce each of the following words *naturally* (or have somebody pronounce them to you). Check the four words that contain neither an unglided nor an r-controlled phoneme.

house; drown

_____ house	_____ drown	_____ young
_____ short	_____ bread	_____ scout
_____ crown	_____ birth	_____ block

scout

crown

_____

*Not all dictionaries and reading instructional materials use this symbol to represent this sound. Some use ä.

Write the two two-letter graphemes that represent this vowel phoneme in each of the four words you checked above.

ou; ow

_____   _____

This vowel sound is called a *diphthong* (dĭf′ thŏng or dĭp′ thông). It is NOT a simple, single phoneme. Originally the word *phthongos* meant "sound" or "voice." And *di-* was a prefix meaning "two."

2; phonemes or sounds

Technically then a diphthong is really [1, 2] vowel _____ in the same syllable that blend or glide together.

Dictionaries uniformly use the pronunciation symbol *ou* to indicate the pronunciation of this phoneme, /aw/.

MINI-REVIEW!

Write *ou* if the underlined letters represent the diphthong *ou*, *ō* if the long *o* sound, or *ŭ* if the short *u* sound.

ou; ŭ; ou

ō; ou; ŭ

ou; ō; ou

th<u>ou</u>sand _____	c<u>ou</u>ntry _____	sh<u>ow</u>ers _____
sn<u>ow</u>ier _____	t<u>ow</u>el _____	r<u>ou</u>gh _____
<u>ou</u>nce _____	will<u>ow</u> _____	cr<u>ow</u>ned _____

Vowel Phonemes: VI

Pronounce each of these words slowly (or have somebody pronounce them to you), possibly even exaggeratedly. Listen carefully. How many vowel phonemes can you detect?

joy   boil   coin   boy

In each word, how many vowel phonemes did you detect that blend or glide together in one syllable?   1   2   3

2

diphthong

These words must contain another [diphthong, phoneme]!

This phoneme is in which of the following words?

oyster; foyer

foible; poignant

_____oyster   _____foyer

_____foible   _____poignant

The pronunciation symbol universally used by American dictionaries to represent this diphthong, /ɔy/, is *oi*.

A possible set of key words for this phoneme is:

joyful hoyden and broiled cloister

What memorable phrase could you create to help you remember this diphthong?

_____

MINI-REVIEW!

If the underlined letters represent the circumflex *o*, write *ô*; if the *ou* diphthong, write *ou*; if the *oi* diphthong, *oi*; AND IF NONE OF THESE, WRITE O. Pay attention to sounds; don't be fooled by letters or spelling patterns!

ô; ô; ou; oi   _____w<u>a</u>ltz   _____fr<u>au</u>d   _____sl<u>ou</u>ch   _____pl<u>oy</u>

ou; ou; O; oi   _____pr<u>ow</u>   _____sauerkr<u>au</u>t   _____<u>a</u>lly   _____gr<u>oi</u>n

Vowel Phonemes: VII and VIII

Do these words contain a total of one or two different vowel phonemes?

1	2	3	4	5	6
book	food	pool	stood	room	wool

2   These words contain [1, 2] different vowel phonemes.

The words with the same vowel sound as in *good* and *cook* are numbers

1; 4; 6   _____, _____, and _____.

This is called the "short double *o*" phoneme. It is represented by the pronunciation symbol o͞o and by the phonemic symbol /u/.

Which of the six words at the top of the page didn't contain the "short double *o*" phoneme? Circle them.

food; pool; room   book   food   pool   stood   room   wool

Which pronunciation symbol do you believe represents this phonemic

o͞o   symbol, /uw/?   o͝o o͞o

What do you think this phoneme is called?

long double *o*   _____short double *o*   _____long double *o*

If a word contains the short double o phoneme, write o͝o; if the long double o, o͞o; AND IF NEITHER, WRITE O.

o͞o; o͞o; o͝o; O   _____loot   _____tune   _____should   _____thousand

o͝o; o͞o; o͝o; O   _____hook   _____new   _____put   _____flood

Several dictionaries use another set of symbols to represent this sound. Read the following respellings and then complete the sentence.

skül   rül   tůk   bůk

ů   The dictionary symbol _____ is also used to represent the o͝o sound

ü   and _____ is used to represent the o͞o sound.

Vowel Phonemes: IX

One dictionary lists 32 different vowel phonemes! However, not all these are important to teachers of reading. The last one we'll investigate is not greatly important—but it occurs very frequently. And it's fairly difficult to discriminate auditorily.

In four of the following words, the underlined letter represents this sound. Challenge: Find these four words! (Pronounce each word naturally.)

pencil; Dakota   _____penc_i_l   _____D_a_kota   _____st_a_mina

bishop; taken   _____bish_o_p   _____l_e_cher   _____tak_e_n

This vowel phoneme is called the *schwa* sound. It is represented by the pronunciation symbol ə and by the phonemic symbol /ə/.

The schwa phoneme sounds something like "uh" and is highly similar to the short *u* sound in *up* and *bun*.

The key words "fam_ou_s sequ_e_l" may help you remember this sound.

Put an X beside each word below in which the underlined letter(s) represent the schwa sound.

genesis; drama   _____gen_e_sis   _____dram_a_   _____mus_i_c

spacious; special   _____spaci_ou_s   _____impeach   _____speci_a_l

Pronounce these words: *actor, helper, calendar.* In many multisyllabic words that end with *or*, *er*, and *ar*, the vowel letter usually represents schwa the _____ sound.

Review #2

Beside each word below, write the pronunciation symbol of the phoneme represented by the underlined letter(s). This symbol is in parenthesis after the name of the phoneme. WRITE O BESIDE ANY WORDS FOR WHICH AN ANSWER IS NOT GIVEN.

short vowel sounds (ă, ĕ, ĭ, ŏ, ŭ)

r-controlled vowel sounds (är, ûr, ôr)

circumflex *o* sound (ô)

ă; är; ô	_____nost<u>a</u>lgia	_____f<u>ar</u>ce	_____<u>au</u>burn
ôr; ĭ; O	_____sn<u>or</u>kle	_____v<u>i</u>sage	_____gr<u>ou</u>ch
ŏ; O; ĕ	_____<u>o</u>ptical	_____sc<u>ou</u>r	_____<u>e</u>thics

```
┌───────────────────────────────┐
│          SCOREBOARD           │
│ I got _____ correct of 9 possible. │
└───────────────────────────────┘
```

Follow the same directions with these phonemes.

ou diphthong (ou)

short double *o* (o͝o)

long double *o* (o͞o)

| ou; o͞o; ou | _____br<u>ow</u>se | _____dr<u>oo</u>p | _____conf<u>ou</u>nd |
| O; o͝o; o͞o | _____wr<u>ou</u>ght | _____sh<u>ou</u>ld | _____rh<u>eu</u>matism |

```
┌───────────────────────────────┐
│          SCOREBOARD           │
│ I got _____ correct of 6 possible. │
└───────────────────────────────┘
```

Repeat with these phonemes.

circumflex *o* (ô)

short double *o* (ŏŏ)

schwa (ə)

O; ŏŏ; ô   _____st<u>u</u>por   _____n<u>oo</u>k   _____sc<u>a</u>ld

ə; ə; ə   _____<u>a</u>bortive   _____civ<u>i</u>l   _____jarg<u>o</u>n

---

SCOREBOARD

So far, I answered _____ correct of 21 possible.

Try to pronounce each word naturally while paying attention to the sound represented by the underlined letter(s). Then write the name and the symbol for each sound. Listen for sounds; don't be fooled by spelling patterns!

	Word	Name of Phoneme	Pronunciation Symbol
long double *o*; ōō	harp<u>oo</u>n	_____	_____
circumflex *o*; ô	fla<u>u</u>nt	_____	_____
short *a*; ă	can<u>a</u>l	_____	_____
short double *o*; ŏŏ (u̇)	c<u>ou</u>ld	_____	_____
schwa; ə	bedl<u>a</u>m	_____	_____
r-controlled; ûr	j<u>our</u>ney	_____	_____
short *i*; ĭ	squ<u>i</u>d	_____	_____
circumflex *o*; ô	alcoh<u>o</u>l	_____	_____
ou diphthong; ou	shr<u>ou</u>d	_____	_____

SCOREBOARD

TOTALLY, of 39 possible,

I answered _____ correctly.

SELF-EVALUATION #2

Check the statement that describes how well you did on Review #2.

I can auditorily distinguish all of the vowel phonemes from each other.

_____ Excellently   _____ Adequately   _____ Poorly

I know the names and symbols of all these vowel phonemes.

_____ Perfectly   _____ Satisfactorily   _____ Confusedly

In light of the above candid evaluation, I should—

_____ continue on with the next section of this book.

_____ quickly review:

_____ the sounds the various phonemes represent.

_____ the names and symbols of the various phonemes.

Long Vowel Phoneme-Grapheme Generalizations

Introduction

So far, we've investigated only sounds. But reading involves more than sounds; it also involves written symbols. A child must learn to "decode" these written symbols if he is to be able to figure out the pronunciation of unknown words.

Because printed words represent oral words, letters can be visual clues to sounds. The letters (graphemes) can signal a reader to make a particular response in attacking an unknown word. Various spelling patterns (letter patterns) in words can be a key to identifying a word. Learning to recognize various morphemes also assists in the process of decoding. (A morpheme is the smallest *meaningful* pronunciation unit.)

Thus written symbols are really just a *code* for oral language. A child who can *crack this code,* who can translate written symbols into already known meaningful oral language, possesses a powerful tool. And that is precisely what *phonics* is all about: knowing which sound(s) each grapheme, morpheme, or spelling pattern represents in an unrecognized word.

One way we teach children to decode words is to show them that, in general, American-English spelling is regular. Phonemes, morphemes, and spelling patterns can frequently be relied upon to indicate certain sounds. That is, the initial grapheme in the unrecognized word *baldric*** invariably represents the same phoneme it does in the known words *baby,* *back,* and *bake.* And there is a high probability that the initial vowel

---

*If you have not previously seen this word yet pronounced it bôl′ drik, you decoded it accurately. Can you figure out what clues or system you used to sound out this strange set of printed symbols?

grapheme in this word, *a*, represents the same vowel phoneme, /ɔ/, that it does in the known word *ball*. Etc. Thus in decoding, the reader correctly and appropriately produces the known and meaningful oral sounds represented by the written symbols.

Therefore, we must teach children to associate certain sounds with certain graphemes and spelling patterns. And then we must teach them to correctly produce these sounds when confronted with the appropriate printed symbol. (In terms of the S-R learning theory, we must teach children to make an appropriate oral response when confronted with certain printed stimuli.)

One prime prerequisite for decoding is to be able to auditorily discriminate one phoneme from another. That is what the section of this book you just finished was all about.

The other prime requisite is to develop memorable associations between certain sounds and their representative graphemes and spelling patterns. That is what the rest of this book is all about.

Long Vowel Phoneme-Grapheme Generalization: I

Can you discover a spelling clue to the long vowel phoneme?

bane	cede	grime	mode	Ute
123	123	123	123	123

long   Each #1 letter represents a [long, short] vowel phoneme.

consonant   Each #2 letter is a [vowel, consonant] letter.

e   Each #3 letter is the vowel letter _____. Linguists call this letter a marker (and educators traditionally call it a "silent" letter) because

does not   it [does, does not] represent a phoneme.

Which spelling pattern do the final three letters of these words follow?

VCe   _____VCC   _____CVC   _____VCe

In VCe words, linguists call the *e* a *marker*. It indicates that the preceding vowel sound is a glided or "long" vowel phoneme.

But consider these words before stating a generalization.

pro m<u>o</u>te'   pa r<u>a</u>de'   sur pr<u>i</u>se'

glided

accented

In these words, the "long" or [glided, unglided] vowel phoneme appears in the [accented, unaccented] syllable.

Generalization time! Use all of the data above to form a generalization that tells about a visual clue to the long vowel sound.

one-

accented

glided

does not

When a [one-, two-] syllable word or a final syllable that is [accented, unaccented] ends in the VCe spelling pattern, the vowel letter usually represents the [glided, unglided] vowel phoneme and the final e [does, does not] represent a sound.

APPLICATION

Pronounce these "nonsense words."*

clope   fline   non drale'   pre strebe'

Which vowel phoneme do you hear in these words?

r<u>u</u>le   fl<u>u</u>te   pr<u>u</u>ne   pl<u>u</u>me

Long double o ($\overline{oo}$)

_____Circumflex o (ô)   _____Long double o ($\overline{oo}$)

All of the words follow the VCe pattern. Why isn't the answer the "long u (ū)"?

The vowel letter u in words with the CVe spelling pattern generally represents one of two sounds. Most current dictionaries and newer reading programs designate the sounds u represents in various ways. Look at the following list to compare the symbols used.

	/yuw/ Pronunciation symbols			/uw/ Pronunciation symbols
mule	ū	y$\overline{oo}$	yü	rule	$\overline{oo}$
cube	ū	y$\overline{oo}$	yü	flute	$\overline{oo}$
fuse	ū	y$\overline{oo}$	yü	prune	$\overline{oo}$

---

*Remember, to a child learning to read, any word he hasn't seen previously (or can't remember seeing before) may be a "nonsense word"—a bunch of visual gibberish that needs to be decoded before it is meaningful or sensible.

The dictionary symbols $y\overline{oo}$, *yü,* and *ū* are used to represent the vowel sound heard in words like *mule, cube,* and *fuse.* Very few words with the CVe spelling pattern and the vowel letter *u* contain a true "long *u*" or glided vowel sound.

Match the dictionary spelling to each of the following words.

1. = c.	1. cute	a. kr$\overline{oo}$d
2. = e.	2. brute	b. hy$\overline{oo}$j
3. = b.	3. huge	c. ky$\overline{oo}$t
4. = f.	4. mute	d. r$\overline{oo}$b
5. = a.	5. crude	e. br$\overline{oo}$t
6. = d.	6. rube	f. my$\overline{oo}$t

Let's find out how much more uncertainty you can stand. Study these words visually and orally.

have   give   come   dove

Yes   Theoretically, should each word contain a long vowel sound? Yes No

short   But in reality, each contains a [long, short] vowel phoneme.

Now pronounce these words.

snare   glare   more   core

In theory, each of these words should also contain a long vowel sound. What letter is the clue that suggests that the words may contain other

r   vowel sounds? _____

It should be clear by this time that many phoneme-grapheme generali-

some   zations have [no, some] exceptions, that they apply only part of the time. This has come to be called their "percent of utility," the extent to which spelling patterns can be relied on to visually signal the correct phoneme. (See Appendix B for some sources listing the frequency with which these generalizations apply.)

Thus we not only need to teach children these generalizations but we must also teach them not to over-rely on them since they are guides and not absolute rules.

Long Vowel Phoneme-Grapheme Generalization: II

maim   bleak   hoax   flay   leech

The first underlined vowel letter in each of the above words represents

glided   a [glided, unglided] phoneme.

And the second vowel letter represents ? phoneme.

no vowel   _____ a short vowel   _____ a long vowel   _____ no vowel

Because they do not represent a sounded phoneme, some educators

silent   call these vowel letters [silent, sounded] letters.

1; 2   In each word, [1, 2] vowel phoneme is represented by [1, 2] vowel

2   letters. In ancient Greek, the prefix _di-_ meant [1, 2] and the base _-graph_

written   meant [sound, written]. Therefore, we have come to call two written

digraph   letters that represent one phoneme a _____.

Before formulating a generalization, study these words.

con ceal′   ob tain′   in deed′

beat′ en   dain′ ty   main′ ly

In these words, the glided vowel phoneme is in the [accented,

accented   unaccented] syllable.

Synthesize all of the above facts.

digraph; one-   When a vowel _____ is in the middle of a [one-, two-]

accented   syllable word or an [accented, unaccented] syllable, the vowel digraph

long or glided   represents a _____ vowel phoneme.

That statement is frequently called the _vowel digraph_ generalization.

And sometimes it is referred to by the abbreviation ?.

CVVC   _____VCCV   _____CVVC   _____CVC

But, as with all products of mankind, this generalization is accurate only part of the time. Put an X in front of any words below that do NOT conform to this generalization.

eight; dread; niece   _____eight   _____dread   _____niece

broad; aisle; ahead   _____broad   _____aisle   _____ahead

many   It is obvious that there are [few, many] exceptions to this generalization!

The five vowel digraphs that conform more consistently than other combinations are found in these words:

br<u>ai</u>se   br<u>ay</u>   cl<u>ea</u>ve   pr<u>ee</u>n   sh<u>oa</u>l

ai; ay; ea; ee; oa   These five digraphs are: _____, _____, _____, _____, _____.

Ideally then, our previous generalization should state:

ai; ay; ea; ee   When one of the vowel digraphs, _____, _____, _____, _____,

oa   or _____, is in the middle of a one-syllable word or an accented syllable,

long or glided   the vowel digraph represents a _____ vowel phoneme.

APPLICATION

Pronounce these "nonsense words" (assuming each follows the above generalization). Hint: They will sound like words you already know.

gload	streat	lait	eest	fayk
keap	nayl	smoak	frait	theez

Long Vowel Phoneme-Grapheme Generalization: III

Put the correct diacritical mark over the underlined vowel letter in each of the following words.

ē; ō; ē; ō; ō; ē   m<u>e</u>   g<u>o</u>   b<u>e</u>   n<u>o</u>   s<u>o</u>   h<u>e</u>

Let's start formulating a generalization.

If a one-syllable word contains only one vowel letter and that vowel letter is at the end of the word, that letter usually represents the

glided or long   _____ vowel phoneme.

(But consider these exceptions: do, to, the.)

Now let's expand this generalization. Pronounce these words.

f<u>i</u>′ nite   b<u>o</u>′ nus   g<u>a</u>′ ble

glided   Each underlined vowel letter represents a [glided, unglided] vowel phoneme.

last; syllable	Furthermore, each is also the [first, last] letter in that [word, syllable]. Such syllables are termed *open syllables*.
is	And each of these syllables [is, is not] accented.
	Now let's put the whole thing together!
accented	If a one-syllable word or an [accented, unaccented] syllable contains only one vowel letter and that vowel letter is at the end of the word
glided	or syllable, that letter usually represents its [glided, unglided] phoneme.

APPLICATION

Put an X in front of each word in which the underlined vowel letter theoretically should follow the above generalization.

mosaic; pugnacious

gradation

_____op′ p<u>o</u> site   _____mo s<u>a</u>′ ic   _____pug n<u>a</u>′ cious

_____gra d<u>a</u>′ tion   _____l<u>o</u> gis′ tics   _____em′ p<u>a</u> thy

Long Vowel Phoneme-Grapheme Generalization: IV

You have now studied the primary generalizations governing long vowel phoneme-grapheme correspondences. Two are of major importance, the VCe generalization and the vowel digraph (or CVVC) generalization. The other one applies much less frequently and is far less useful in decoding unrecognized words.

But there are three spelling patterns that are helpful in decoding even though they are of too infrequent applicability to be called generalizations. They are illustrated in the following words.

light   find   mold

might   kind   bold

glided or long

In each word, the single vowel letter in the middle of a one-syllable word stands for the _____ phoneme.

The three graphemic bases in which this phoneme occurs are *-ight*,

-ind, -old

_____, and _____.

List as many words as you can for each of the following graphemic bases.*

-ight	-ind	-old
_____	_____	_____
_____	_____	_____
_____	_____	_____
_____	_____	_____
_____	_____	_____
_____	_____	_____
_____	_____	_____

Review #3

This completes our study of the generalizations governing long vowel phoneme-grapheme correspondence. To help you remember what you have learned, complete the following generalizations FROM MEMORY. Answers are upside down at the bottom of the next page.

Directions: Study the group of words beside each number. Decide which generalization they represent. Then complete the generalization.

1. prime   sane   hone   pro pose´   a muse´

    When a one-syllable word or an _____ final syllable ends in the _____ spelling pattern, the vowel letter usually represents its _____ vowel _____ and the final _____ does _____ represent a sound.

2. re frain´   poach   stray   seep   cleave   can teen´

    When one of these five vowel _____—_____, _____, _____, _____, or _____—is in the _____ of a one-_____ word or an _____ syllable, the vowel digraph represents a _____ vowel phoneme.

---

*There are hundreds of other graphemic bases. Some are: *-ain*, *-ick*, *-an*, *-est*, *-orn*, *-un*, *-are*, etc.

3. be   he   go   ra′ dar   cli′ max

If a one-syllable word or an [accented, unaccented] syllable contains only one vowel letter and that vowel letter is at the _____ of the _____ or _____, that letter usually represents a _____ vowel phoneme.

SELF-EVALUATION #3

_____ Yahhh!   _____ Ho hum   _____ #@*?&!

Other Vowel Phoneme-Grapheme Generalizations

Short Vowel Generalization: I

What visual clues in each of these words indicate which vowel phoneme is represented by the underlined vowel letter?

j<u>a</u>b   g<u>e</u>m   d<u>i</u>n   p<u>o</u>d   h<u>u</u>t

short   Each word contains a [short, glided] vowel phoneme.

CHALLENGE: Words with this spelling pattern are often called ?

CVC   words. _____VCV _____CVC

If a syllable ending with a vowel phoneme (f<u>a</u>' vor, sc<u>i</u>' ence) is called an *open* syllable, then a CVC syllable ending with one or more

closed   consonant phonemes (ban' ter, crun<u>ch</u>) must be called a _____ syllable.

Before formulating a generalization, consider the phoneme in these words: f<u>o</u>s' sil   st<u>a</u>m' in a   d<u>i</u>s' mal

unglided   In these words the short or [glided, unglided] vowel phoneme is
accented   in an [accented, unaccented] CVC syllable.

Now synthesize the above information.

---
vowel; CVC   When a single _____ letter is in a [CVC, VCV] spelling

one-; accented   pattern, either in a [one-, two-] syllable word or an [accented, unaccented]

unglided   syllable, that letter usually represents its [glided, unglided] or short vowel phoneme.

APPLICATION

Mark each underlined vowel letter in these "nonsense" words with a breve (˘) and then pronounce each one correctly.

b<u>o</u>d' fer   cr<u>a</u>nd   sm<u>e</u>ss   pl<u>u</u>ch   gr<u>i</u>x' ten

	Grapheme	Phonemic Symbol	Pronuncia-tion Symbol
	ou and *ow*	/aw/	ou

diphthong

ou

The graphemes *ou* and *ow* usually represent the vowel [diphthong, digraph] /aw/ which is represented by the pronunciation symbol [ou, ow, aw].

NUMBER TWO

re<u>joi</u>ce	trape<u>zoi</u>d	p<u>oi</u>se
depl<u>oy</u>	ann<u>oy</u>	Fl<u>oy</u>d

	Grapheme	Phonemic Symbol	Pronuncia-tion Symbol
	oi and *oy*	/ɔy/	oi

thong

oi

The graphemes *oi* and *oy* usually represent the vowel diph _ _ _ _ _ /ɔy/ which is represented by the pronunciation symbol [oi, oy].

APPLICATION

These "nonsense" words will sound like real words if pronounced correctly using the *ou* or the *oi* phoneme.

dout	enjoi	clowd	croud
oyl	oister	lowd	avoyd

Double *O* Generalization

What would you do if you came across this sentence containing two words you didn't immediately recognize?

The *plood strook* was in the corner.

Did you rhyme *plood* with *good* or *food*?

_____good   _____food

Did you rhyme *strook* with *book* or *spook*?

_____book   _____spook

Regrettably, either pronunciation would have been acceptable. There is no generalization that satisfactorily predicts whether a reader should try the "short double *o*" phoneme ($\breve{oo}$ or *u̇*) or the "long double *o*" phoneme ($\overline{oo}$ or *ü*) when he sees the *oo* grapheme in an unrecognized word.

Rather than a generalization, we teach a strategy. The "long double *o*" phoneme occurs almost twice as frequently as does the "short double *o*" phoneme so we teach children to do this.

If a one-syllable word or an accented syllable contains the *oo* grapheme, try the "long double *o*" phoneme as in *pool* and *room*.

If you don't recognize this pronunciation, try the "short double *o*" phoneme as in *stood* and *hook*.

APPLICATION

These "nonsense" words will sound like real words if you use the correct "double *o*" phoneme in them. Write $\overline{oo}$ if it should be the "long double *o*," $\breve{oo}$ if the "short double *o*."

$\overline{oo}$; $\breve{oo}$; $\overline{oo}$; $\overline{oo}$ _____rool   _____shood   _____assoom   _____conclood

$\breve{oo}$; $\overline{oo}$; $\breve{oo}$; $\breve{oo}$.   _____poot   _____floot   _____poosh   _____pooding

Schwa Generalization

Do you remember what vowel phoneme the underlined letters represent in the following words?

       <u>a</u>bout   tak<u>e</u>n   penc<u>i</u>l   gall<u>o</u>p   circ<u>u</u>s

It represents the /ə/ phoneme and is called the **?** sound.

schwa   _____glided   _____schwa   _____circumflex

What are some visual signals that tell us when it occurs? Examine these words.

       <u>a</u> larm′   di′<u>e</u>t   por′ p<u>oi</u>se   re′ g<u>io</u>n   per′ il <u>ou</u>s

May numerous vowel letters and letter combinations represent this

Yes   phoneme?   Yes   No

Does it seem to occur in accented or unaccented syllables?*

unaccented

_____accented   _____unaccented

Complete this generalization.

unaccented

A vowel letter or cluster in an [accented, unaccented] syllable usually

schwa; /ə/

represents the _____ phoneme, [/ə/, /aw/].

In each of the following "nonsense" words, underline the vowel letter or letters that represent the schwa phoneme.

pigt<u>a</u>nce; sult<u>ai</u>n

                pig′ tance   sul′ tain

dolt<u>u</u>m; brit<u>ou</u>s

                dol′ tum   bri′ tous

aplont; skog<u>io</u>n

                a plont′   sko′ gion

Spell these words correctly by replacing the pronunciation symbol ə with the correct letters. The first one is done for you.

famous	ballət	(ballot)	faməs	_____
chorus; civil	chorəs	_____	civəl	_____
canoe; sergeant	cənoe	_____	sergənt	_____
among; official	əmong	_____	əfficəl	_____

Review #4

Complete the following vowel phoneme-grapheme generalizations FROM MEMORY. Answers are on page 36.

Directions: Study the group of words beside each number. Decide which generalization they represent. Then complete the generalization.

1. brunt   jell   mim′ ic   pros′ pect

When a single _____ letter is in a _____ spelling pattern, either in a _____-syllable word or an _____ syllable, that letter usually represents its _____ or _____ vowel _____.

---

*One current dictionary designates the vowel sound in words such as *cut, trunk,* and *ulcer* as the schwa sound. According to this reference, one-syllable words and accented syllables as well as unaccented syllables may contain the schwa sound.

2. act   ebb   is′ sue   oc′ cu py

   When a single _____ letter is the _____ letter in
   a _____ syllable, either in a _____-syllable word or an
   _____ syllable, that letter usually represents its
   _____ or _____ vowel _____.

3. sauce   brawn   daunt′ less   awn′ ing

   When the letter _____ is immediately followed by a _____ or
   _____, either in a _____-_____ word or an
   _____ _____, that letter usually represents the
   _____ _____ phoneme.

4. bound   cow′ ard   vow′ els   moun′ tain

   The graphemes _____ and _____ usually represent the vowel
   _____ /aw/ which is represented by the pronunciation
   symbol _____.

5. loi′ ter   poi′ son   roy′ al   voy′ age

   The graphemes _____ and _____ usually represent the vowel
   _____ /ɔy/ which is represented by the pronunciation
   symbol _____.

6. booth   doo′ dle   hood   book′ let

   If a _____-_____ word or an _____
   _____ contains the _____ grapheme, try the
   _____ _____ _____ phoneme as in *pool* and *room*.
   If you don't recognize this pronunciation, try the _____
   _____ _____ phoneme as in _____ and
   _____.

7. pla toon′   hand′ some   junc′ tion   pi′ ous   vil′ lain

   A _____ letter or cluster in an _____ syllable
   usually represents the _____ phoneme, /ə/.

REVIEW #4: ANSWERS

1. When a single <u>vowel</u> letter is in a <u>CVC</u> spelling pattern, either in a <u>one</u>-syllable word or an <u>accented</u> syllable, that letter usually represents its <u>unglided</u> or <u>short</u> vowel <u>phoneme</u>.

2. When a single <u>vowel</u> letter is the <u>first</u> letter in a <u>closed</u> syllable, either in a <u>one</u>-syllable word or an <u>accented</u> syllable, that letter usually represents its <u>unglided</u> or <u>short</u> vowel <u>phoneme</u>.

3. When the letter <u>a</u> is immediately followed by a <u>u</u> or a <u>w</u>, either in a <u>one-syllable</u> word or an <u>accented</u> <u>syllable</u>, that letter usually represents the <u>circumflex</u> <u>o</u> phoneme.

4. The graphemes <u>ou</u> and <u>ow</u> usually represent the vowel <u>diphthong</u> /aw/ which is represented by the pronunciation symbol <u>ou</u>.

5. The graphemes <u>oi</u> and <u>oy</u> usually represent the vowel <u>diphthong</u> /ɔy/ which is represented by the pronunciation symbol <u>oi</u>.

6. If a <u>one-syllable</u> word or an <u>accented</u> <u>syllable</u> contains the <u>oo</u> grapheme try the "<u>long</u> <u>double</u> <u>o</u>" phoneme as in *pool* and *room*.

    If you don't recognize this pronunciation, try the "<u>short</u> <u>double</u> <u>o</u>" phoneme as in <u>stood</u> and <u>hook</u> (or other o͝o words).

7. A <u>vowel</u> letter or cluster in an <u>unaccented</u> syllable usually represents the <u>schwa</u> phoneme, /ə/.

SELF-EVALUATION #4

_____ WHEE!

_____ O.K.

_____ Do not pass Go. Do not collect $200!

Consonant Phonemes

Introduction

The simplicity of consonant phonemes and their graphemic representations should be a welcome relief after the complexity of vowel phonemes and graphemes! One thing making them simpler is that consonant sounds are usually more auditorily distinguishable from each other. The second is that the principle phoneme-grapheme correspondences are much more regular, much more consistent! When you see the letter *o* in a word, it can easily represent or help represent, eight separate vowel phonemes! But most consonant letters usually represent only one phoneme, no matter where in the word the letter occurs.

The 21 consonant letters, either singly or in combination, represent only 26 different phonemes.* Eighteen of these 21 letters are phonemically consistent and invariant. That is, whenever they represent a phoneme by themselves and not in combination with other letters, they represent the same phoneme no matter whether they are in an initial, medial, or final position in a word, e.g., <u>b</u>ound, ro<u>b</u>ot, or dra<u>b</u>.

Therefore, even though there are many more consonant graphemes than vowel graphemes, consonant phonemes and phoneme-grapheme relationships are much easier for elementary school pupils to learn and remember than are their vowel counterparts. And they should be equivalently easier for you, too.

But lest you be lulled into a false sense of security about the simplicity of consonants, answer this question. If the "long *a* sound" is pronounced "ay" and if the "short *a* sound" is pronounced approximately "aah," what sound does the letter *b* represent in our language?

---

*Different dictionaries may list slightly varying numbers of vowel and consonant phonemes because linguists don't totally agree as to how many sounds there are in American-English.

_____The "bee" sound

_____The "buh" sound

_____Neither of the above seems correct!

"Neither of the above . . ." is the right answer.

"Bee" is obviously incorrect. For *bat,* we don't say /bē-at/ nor for *book,* /bē-o͞ok/.

Similarly for *bell,* we don't say /buh-ell/ nor for *bite,* /buh-īt/.

If we did, we would not be pronouncing them as the one-syllable words they are. Rather, we would be pronouncing them as two-syllable words; we would be adding an extra syllable.

But what then, for heaven's sake, is the sound represented by *b*?

The answer is that, when spoken naturally in a word, the consonant phoneme of *b* blends almost inseparably with the vowel or consonant phoneme following it. It is extremely difficult, if not impossible, to isolate this sound.

The same is true for other consonant phonemes, particularly these.

c in cantankerous	*j* in jeopardy
d in decrepit	*k* in kindred
g in gullable	*p* in pernicious

You may have heard people—perhaps even your teachers in elementary school—say that *b* represents the "buh" sound. This is not only inaccurate but it is harmful to children trying to decode unrecognized words because they will add a superfluous syllable to these words—as we already discovered.

What then do we tell children about consonant phonemes?

One, we make sure they can auditorily distinguish between /bit/ and /pit/, between /bent/ and /dent/, etc. And then we tell them that *b* represents the sound heard at the beginning of /bit/ and /bent/ or the end of /lob/ and /glib/. But we try NOT to isolate this sound for them, we try NOT to tell them that *b* represents the "buh" sound.

Two, with some consonant phonemes represented by letters other than those above, we can artificially elongate the sound, for example, we can say *m* represents the sound heard at the end of *hum-m-m-m* or at the beginning of *m-m-m-monkey*. It is tricky for teachers to master this; it is ever so much simpler to say "*m* represents the muh sound."

This technique of elongating the consonant phoneme seems to work best with the sounds commonly represented by the letters in these words.

f in facsimile and whiff

l in loath and null

m in morsel and doom

n in nomadic and bacon

r in rancid and donor

s in sedate and caress

v in vortex and swerve

z in zodiac and jazz

Say each of the above words several times using this "elongated enunciation" technique. Try it until you get the feel of it, until you believe elementary school pupils would be able to clearly hear these sounds as you pronounce them and even emulate your enunciation.

Consonant Phonemes: I

One reason consonant phonemes are simpler to learn than are vowel phonemes is that there are almost no new pronunciation symbols, terms, or diacritical marks to learn.

For all practical purposes, the pronunciation symbol for each consonant phoneme is merely its alphabetical letter.

The pronunciation entry for *bad* is merely (băd), for *slump*, (slŭmp), for *church*, (chûrch), etc.

For each single consonant letter, write the phoneme it represents, and create a memorable key phrase that will help you—and possibly later, some elementary school pupils—better remember it.

	Consonant Letter	Consonant Phoneme	
	b	/b/	Bold Billy Batson
/d/	d	/ /	_____
/f/	f	/ /	_____
/h/	h	/ /	_____
/j/	j	/ /	_____
/k/	k	/ /	_____
/l/	l	/ /	_____
/m/	m	/ /	_____
/n/	n	/ /	_____
/p/	p	/ /	_____
/r/	r	/ /	_____
/t/	t	/ /	_____
/v/	v	/ /	_____
/w/	w	/ /	_____
/z/	z	/ /	_____

Consonant Phonemes: II

How many phonemes do the underlined letters represent in each word?

braggart   flamboyant   profane   scoundrel   twitch

Two   _____One   _____Two   _____Unable to tell

The untrained ear (yours?) may detect only one phoneme but there are definitely two. The phonemes *blend* together so smoothly as to be

blend   virtually inseparable. This type of consonant is called a consonant bl___. Another common term is consonant cluster.

Listen carefully to these words: sprawl straggle

3	In each of these words there are [2, 3] underlined consonant gra-
3	phemes. And these three letters represent a total of [1, 2, 3] consonant sounds.
	Therefore, *each* underlined consonant letter in sprawl and in straggle
1	represents only [1, 2, 3] phoneme.

Circle the initial blends in each word below. Then complete the sentence that tells how the blends are classified.

bl; cl; fl; gl; pl; sl; spl	blurt clutch flaw glutton plead slush spleen
l	These blends all contain the letter _____ and are therefore called
l	_____-blends.
br; cr; dr; fr; gr; pr	bravo cringe droll fret grudge prime
scr; spr; str; thr; tr	scrimp spree strut thrash trance
r	These blends all contain the letter _____ and are therefore called
r	_____-blends.
sc; scr; sk; sl; sn; sp	scathe scrawl skit slouch snipe sperm
spl; spr; st; str; sw	splice spruce stern strum swarm
s	These blends all contain the letter _____ and are therefore called
s	_____-blends.

SUMMARY

The three main groups of consonant blends are:

1. The _____-blends.

2. The _____-blends.

3. The _____-blends.

Now study these phonetic respellings: kwēn   kwĭk   kwōt

qu	In spelling, all of these words begin with the *letters* [kw, qu]. Therefore,
2	the grapheme *qu* represents [1, 2] consonant phonemes. So we commonly
cluster	call the grapheme *qu* a consonant blend or a consonant _____.

All the consonant blends just studied occurred at the beginning of words. Circle the consonant blends in the following words. (Can one word contain two blends?)

nt; lt; ct; ft	taint	lilt	pact	sift
nd; mp; ld; sk	tend	tramp	weld	disk
lk; nk; mp; st	bilk	fink	clump	lust
ld; tr; str-nt; cl	bold	patrol	instrument	seclude

From the above examples and those on the previous page, we can

numerous; blends   conclude that there are [few, numerous] consonant _____ or

clusters.

3   And it is also obvious that consonant blends can occur in [1, 2, 3]

final   positions in words, initial, medial, or _____.

Even though we frequently teach children a different key word phrase
for each separate blend, it is obvious that there are far too many blends
for us to write such a phrase for each one. However, you might like
to write ones for some of the more common blends.

bl	A bloody black block
cr	_____
sp	_____
pl	_____
str	_____

Consonant Phonemes: III

Compare the sounds heard at the beginning of each pair of words.
Write B by all words in which the underlined graphemes represent a
consonant blend and O by those in which they don't.

O;B;O;O   _____chop   _____stone   _____thin   _____whip

B;O;B;B   _____crop   _____shone   _____skin   _____flip

Write the underlined consonant letters in the above words that do
not represent consonant blends.

ch;sh;th;wh   _____   _____   _____   _____

How many consonant phonemes does *ch* seem to represent?

1;1;1;1   1 2   *sh*? 1 2   *th*? 1 2   *wh*? 1 2

2

1   Contrary to consonant blends, the [1, 2] consonant letters represent only [1, 2] consonant sound.

Previously we learned that two vowel letters representing one vowel phoneme are called a *vowel digraph*. Therefore, two consonant letters representing one consonant phoneme must be called a consonant

digraph   _____.

Many combinations of letters are sometimes classified as consonant digraphs. Among these are the following.

ng in throng	*ck* in slack	*ph* in epitaph
gh in enough	*qu* in oblique	

However, we typically only emphasize these four consonant digraphs: *ch*, *sh*, *th*, and *wh*.

Of these, *sh* and *wh* represent standard phonemes which are pronounced essentially the same in all words.

Reading instructional materials and dictionaries use the pronunciation symbol *sh* to represent the first phoneme, /sh/ as in *she* and *show*. But the first phoneme in *what* and *when* is not represented by the pronunciation symbol *wh*.

If you listen carefully as you pronounce *what, when, wheel,* and *white,* you may be able to detect that there is the beginning of a sound preceding

/h/   the /w/. This sound is the [/h/, /ə/, /v/] phoneme.

Since /h/ precedes /w/ in the pronunciation, it is logical that the first phoneme in *what* and *when* be represented by the pronunciation

hw; hw   symbol [wh, hw]. And *wheel* and *white* are phonetically spelled __ēl

hw   and __īt.

But the digraphs *ch* and *th* represent more than just one phoneme.

The *ch* digraph usually represents the phoneme /ch/ heard at the beginning of *chapel, chirp,* and *churn*. This phoneme is represented by

ch   the pronunciation symbol [tch, s, ch].

Occasionally, *ch* represents the initial phoneme in *chaos, chemical,* and *character,* /k/.

Infrequently *ch* represents the /sh/ phoneme as in *chiffon,* *champagne,* and *machine.*

Last, we come to the *th* digraph. Pronounce the words in these two rows.

1. th<u>ing</u>   <u>th</u>umb   <u>th</u>ought   <u>th</u>ank
2. <u>th</u>ese   <u>th</u>at   <u>th</u>em   <u>th</u>ey

How many different phonemes are represented by the *th* digraph in these words?   1 2 3 Unable to tell.

> **2**

All the words in row 1 begin with one phoneme while those in row 2 begin with another.

Dictionaries uniformly use the pronunciation symbol *th* to represent the initial phoneme in *thing, thumb, thought,* and *thank.*

And they commonly use one of these pronunciation symbols to represent the initial phoneme in *these, that, them,* and *they: th* or *ŦH.* We will use *ŦH.*

Can you accurately discriminate these two phonemes? Write *th* in front of words in which the *th* represents the phoneme in *thing* and *thought* and *ŦH* in front of those in which it represents the phoneme in *them* and *that.*

> ŦH; ŦH; th
>
> ŦH; th; ŦH
>
> th; th; ŦH

_____their   _____thus   _____ba<u>th</u>

_____ba<u>th</u>e   _____faith   _____mo<u>th</u>er

_____<u>th</u>atch   _____<u>th</u>eme   _____la<u>th</u>er

What causes the difference between the pronunciation of these two distinct phonemes? Hold your finger tips about one inch in front of your mouth and use the "elongated enunciation" technique you learned earlier in this section on the initial phoneme as you pronounce *thin* and *thunder.*

> **Yes**

Did you feel expelled air on your finger tips?   Yes No

Now repeat these words with your fingers on your voice box.

Did you feel your voice box slightly (and feel your tongue vibrate slightly also)?   Yes No

> **No**

Because *no* sound is produced in the creation of the /th/ phoneme,

it is called a [voiceless, voiced] phoneme.

Now repeat the process (fingers in front of mouth and on voice box) with these words: *there* and *those.*

Because much less air was expelled and a definite rumble or vibration was created in the voice box and by the tongue, the /ᵮH/ phoneme

is called a [voiced, voiceless] phoneme.

Even though there is not a generalization concerning the phoneme-grapheme correspondence for these two phonemes, the voiceless phoneme /th/ occurs far more frequently, possibly ten times so, than does the voiced phoneme /ᵮH/.

Feeling resourceful? Create a phrase to help you remember each of these phonemes!

th _____   ᵮH _____

There are many consonant letter clusters that appear to meet the definition of a consonant digraph. That is, two letters that represent one phoneme. Three of these are in rhapsody, knave, and wrath.

But because one of these letters does not represent a phoneme, they

are generally not classified as consonant [letters, digraphs].

On the line by each word, write the letter than represents the sound heard in the underlined letter combination.

gnome _____   knurl _____

writhe _____   rhythm _____

solemn _____   aplomb _____

Other such consonant letter combinations occur occasionally as in these words. Circle the letter that represents the phoneme in each underlined letter combination.

khaki   science   sign

psychology   diaphragm   pseudo

aisle   pneumonia   ghost

Consonant Phoneme-Grapheme Generalization: I

Seventeen consonant letters are considered phonemically consistent. That is, most of the time when one of these letters, by itself and not in combination with other letters, represents a phoneme, it represents

the same [the same, a different] sound. For example, in the word *maximum,* the

3 consonant letter *m* occurs [2, 3, 4] times, in the initial, medial, and

the same final positions. And each time it represents [the same, a different] sound. The single consonant letters to which this generalization best applies are:

b	d	f	h	j	k
l	m	n	p	q	r
t	v	w	y	z	

The four single consonant letters that don't follow this consistent

g; s; x sound-letter relationship are *c*, ____, ____, and ____. Each generally represents two phonemes.

2; /k/ In *circus* (sûr′ kəs), *c* represents [1, 2] phonemes, /s/ and / /.

2; /j/ In *geography* (jē ŏg′ rə fē), *g* represents [1, 2] phonemes, / / and /g/.

2; /z/ In *season* (sē′ zən), *s* represents [1, 2] phonemes, /s/ and / /.

/z/ In *exact* (ĕg zăkt′), *x* represents two phonemes, /g/ and / /, each

2 in a separate syllable. And in *expect* (ĕk spĕkt′), *x* represents [1, 2]

/k/; /s/ phonemes, / / and / /, both of which are in separate syllables. While

2 in *sex* (sĕks), it again represents [1, 2] phonemes but both are in the same syllable.

Thus we are able to teach children that whenever any of these 17 consonant letters occurs by itself in a word, it will probably represent the same phoneme or the same sound value.

Even though we spend an enormous amount of time in beginning reading instruction teaching each of these single consonant phoneme-grapheme correspondences to children, we will assume it is unnecessary to do likewise with you.

However, we have not comprehensively nor exhaustively studied the topic; rather we have surveyed it. There are numerous although *infrequent* consonant phoneme-grapheme correspondences we haven't mentioned. Some of these are as follows:

Letter	Sound
d	/j/ as in indiv<u>d</u>ual
f	/v/ as in o<u>f</u>
x	/z/ as in <u>x</u>ylophone
g	/zh/ as in mira<u>g</u>e
s	/sh/ as in <u>s</u>ugar
q	/k/ as in uni<u>qu</u>e

We have included only the basics that you will need to *begin* teaching decoding to elementary school pupils.

Consonant Phoneme-Grapheme Generalizations: II and III

We studied some consonant phonemes in the previous lessons. Now we'll investigate some visual clues as to which sound(s) children should think or produce when they see certain consonant letters in an unrecognized word.

As you pronounce the words in each row, pay attention to the phoneme represented by the grapheme *c*.

1. <u>c</u>redence   <u>c</u>ulinary   <u>c</u>ogitate   <u>c</u>lairvoyance
2. <u>c</u>itadel   <u>c</u>entaur   <u>c</u>ynical   <u>c</u>ephalic

Check one *or more* of the following that describe the above situation.

_____Two different phonemes are represented by the *c*.

_____The letters following *c* determine which phoneme the letter *c* represents.

_____Sometimes *c* represents the /k/ sound, sometimes the /s/ sound.

All of the above.   _____All of the above.

/s/   In row 2, *c* represents the phoneme [/k/, /s/]. This phoneme is commonly called the *soft c* sound and is represented in dictionary respellings

s   by the pronunciation symbol [k, c, s].

e; i   The letter immediately following the *c* is either an _____, an _____,

y   or a _____.

GENERALIZE!

e; i   When the grapheme *c* is followed by the letter _____, or _____, or

y; soft *c*   _____, it usually represents the _____ _____ phoneme that is

s   frequently also spelled by the letter [c, k, s] as in *soon* and *seem*.

Now study these words, visually and auditorily.

bicycle   lucid   sauce   spicy   decimal   facet

This generalization works as well in the middle of a word as it does

True   at the beginning.   True   False

Now examine these words.

clamor   cranial   fac' tion   pact

collaborate   caress   stat' ic   sac' ro sanct

/k/   In these words, the grapheme *c* represents the phoneme [/k/, /s/].

i   And in none of these words is the letter *c* followed by an *e*, _____, or

y   _____.

If the /s/ sound *c* represents is called the *soft c,* then it is reasonable

hard   that the /k/ sound *c* represents will be called the _____ *c* sound

k   and that the pronunciation symbol [s, k] will be used.

Complete this generalization about this sound *c* represents.

i   When the grapheme *c* is followed by any letter other than *e*, _____,

y; last or final   or _____, or when it is the _____ letter in a word or syllable,

/k/   it usually represents the [/k/, /s/] phoneme. It is frequently called

hard   the _____ *c* sound.

APPLICATION!

Write S before a "nonsense" word if the underlined *c* represents the *soft c* sound, /s/. Write H if it represents the *hard c* sound, /k/.

H; S; S; H ⎯⎯⎯c̲lemter ⎯⎯⎯c̲elmter ⎯⎯⎯ telmc̲er ⎯⎯⎯meltrec̲

Consonant Phoneme-Grapheme Generalization: IV

How many phonemes does the grapheme *g* represent in the following

2 words? 1 2 3 Unable to tell

1. galaxy glutton gorge grope dogma
2. gyrate gingerly gender rage suggest

The phoneme represented by *g* in row 1 is commonly called the *hard*

soft *g* sound; that in row 2 is typically called the ⎯⎯⎯⎯⎯ *g* sound.

Using the information you learned from the previous lesson on the *hard* and *soft* sounds that *c* represents and from your examination of the above words, complete this generalization.

e; i When the grapheme *g* is followed by the letter ⎯⎯, or ⎯⎯,* or

y; soft *g* ⎯⎯, it usually represents the ⎯⎯⎯⎯⎯⎯ sound that is also

j spelled by the letter [g, j]. When it is followed by any other letter in

hard *g* a word or a syllable, it represents the ⎯⎯⎯⎯⎯⎯ sound.

Dictionary pronunciation keys represent the *hard g* sound by the pronunciation symbol *g* and the *soft g* sound by the pronunciation symbol

j [g, j].

APPLICATION!

Write S before a "nonsense" word if the underlined *g* represents the *soft g* sound, /j/. Write H if it represents the *hard g* sound, /g/.

H; S; H ⎯⎯⎯glenpod ⎯⎯⎯gelnpod ⎯⎯⎯delngop

H ⎯⎯⎯delnpog

⎯⎯⎯⎯⎯⎯⎯⎯⎯⎯⎯

*Because there are so many exceptions to words beginning with *gi-* (*gift, gingham, girl, give*) and so few words in which y follows *g*, it might be best if we limited this generalization only to *ge-* words. Regrettably most traditional programs don't limit this generalization. In the past, they have taught children the whole (misleading) principle.

Consonant Phoneme-Grapheme Generalization: V

The only other consonant phoneme-grapheme generalization of consequence can be observed in the following words and their dictionary respellings.

hallow—hăl′ ō	fritter —frĭt′ ər
bailiff —bā′ lif	sorrowfully—sŏr′ ə fəl ē

CHALLENGE

With no additional information, complete this generalization.

single   In a doubled consonant grapheme, the two letters usually represent a [single, double] consonant sound.

Without this generalization, how would these words be pronounced?

stopped   stirred

1   With the generalization, each has only [1, 2] syllable; without it,
2   both would have [1, 2] syllables.

And without this generalization, words such as *letter* and *warrior* could be pronounced quite unnaturally by children learning to decode unrecognized words.

But look and listen carefully to these "exceptions."

accident   suggest

c; g   These seeming exceptions can be explained on the basis of the hard—soft sounds that _____ and _____ represent, the sounds that you have just studied.

And finally, look at these words and their phonetic respellings.

mission—mĭsh′ ən   passion—păsh′ ən

/sh/   If *ss* is followed by *ion*, *ss* represents the [/s/, /sh/] phoneme and is an exception to the "doubled consonant" generalization.

Review #5

1. Compared with a single vowel grapheme, a single consonant grapheme
fewer   typically represents [fewer, more] phonemes.

2. Why shouldn't we tell children that *m* represents the "muh" sound?

_____A. They will get it confused with the name of the letter.

B   _____B. It produces an extra syllable in sounding out words.

3. Write B before a word if the underlined letters represent a consonant blend. Write D if they represent a consonant digraph.

B; D; D   _____scanty   _____thatch   _____chauvanist

D; B; D   _____lethargy   _____dolt   _____wheeze

D; B; B   _____shuttle   _____appraise   _____splurge

1   4. In a consonant blend *each* grapheme represents [1, 2] phoneme.

1   5. In a consonant digraph two letters represent only [1, 2] [phoneme,

phoneme   grapheme].

6. Write the pronunciation symbol used in dictionary respellings for the

hw   digraph in when. _____

7. Check the words in which the *th* digraph represents the voiceless phoneme /th/.

thud; cathode; uncouth   _____thud   _____cathode   _____uncouth

8. Write 1 before the following "nonsense" words in which the underlined *c* or *g* grapheme represents the *soft sound*. Write 2 if it represents the *hard sound*.

1; 1; 1   _____spargin   _____moorcy   _____ceaming

2; 2; 2   _____galbane   _____toglic   _____recshun

9. How many phonemes do the underlined letters represent in stubble,

1   offense, and fatally?   1   2

SELF-EVALUATION #5

_____Excellent   _____Good   _____HELP!!!

Structural Analysis

Introduction

Trying to decode, letter by letter, words such as *enchantment* and *formaldehyde* would be:

_____ slow and tedious

_____ frustrating

_____ probably impossible

_____ All of the above.

All of the above.

Children must learn to see—and pronounce—meaningful "chunks" of words: graphemic bases, syllables, compound words, contractions, prefixes, suffixes, and inflectional endings. This is typically called structural analysis.

The various structural analysis skills encompass a decoding system based on the recognition of the larger, more meaningful "chunks" of words. Structural analysis skills span all levels in today's reading programs. Early in the first grade in some programs, students are exposed to various inflectional endings. And prefixes and suffixes, usually introduced in the second grade, are studied far beyond the elementary school level. The development of such skills is a vital part of the reading process. The *decoding* (reading) process is most effective when the beginning reader combines phonic analysis skills—covered in the first part of this book— with structural analysis skills—which the last section of the book is all about.

Inflectional Ending Generalization: I

Study these word pairs.

stride	ooze	smudge
striding	oozing	smudging

does not	In each case the final *e* [does, does not] represent a sound.
	And the final *e* was dropped before the inflectional ending *-ing* was
added	_____ to the base word.
	Examine the following word "equations."

$$evade + ed = evaded$$
$$ledge + er = ledger$$
$$crude + est = crudest$$

Why aren't the inflected forms of these words spelled *evadeed, ledgeer,* and *crudeest?*

e; dropped	It's because the final _____ of the base word was [dropped, added]
added	before the inflectional ending was _____.
	The inflectional endings *-ing, -ed, -er,* and *-es* all begin with a [vowel,
vowel	consonant] letter.
	Complete this generalization.
e	When a base word ends with a final _____, drop the *e* before adding
vowel	an inflectional ending beginning with a [vowel, consonant] letter.

COMMENT

This is a *spelling,* not a reading, generalization! In the above form, this generalization tells how to form an inflected word from a base word. It does NOT tell how to decode an inflected word!

This spelling generalization is most effective when we teach children to decode words. We teach them this generalization and show them examples. Then we give them inflected words and tell them to find or write the base word. The base word can be the key to decoding unfamiliar words.

Find the base words in these examples.

grope	1. groping—grop grope
chide	2. chides— _____

Inflectional Ending Generalization: II

What happened in the following word pairs? Why?

flag	slim	smug	plod
flagged	slimmer	smuggest	plodding

consonant   The final [consonant, vowel] letter was doubled before an inflectional ending (or a suffix) was added.

Why?

CHALLENGE

Complete this generalization.

CVC
consonant
vowel

When the last three letters of a base word end with the [VCV, CVC] spelling pattern, double the final [consonant, vowel] letter before adding an inflectional ending (or a suffix) beginning with a [consonant, vowel] letter.

spelling   The above generalization is stated as a [reading, spelling] rule.

Therefore, to help children see base words, we have students circle the base words in inflected word forms. You do this in the following words.

combat; shred; prim; war
dog; metal; glad; shred

combatting	shredded	primmest	warrior
dogged	metallic	gladden	shredding

Now, apply your skills to the following "nonsense" words.

trup; snib; flot; brum

truppery	snibbed	flottest	brumming

Inflectional Ending Generalization: III

What spelling generalization is evident in these word pairs?

rally	fury	envy	thrifty	quarry
rallied	furious	enviable	thriftiest	quarrying

CHALLENGE!

Complete this generalization with no more data than what you learned from studying the above words and from the previous two lessons.

	When a base word ends with the letter _____ preceded by a
y	[consonant, vowel] letter, change the *y* to _____ before adding an
consonant; i	inflectional ending (or a suffix) beginning with a [vowel, consonant]
vowel	letter—other than *-ing*.

Is this a reading or a spelling generalization?

Spelling   _____ Reading   _____ Spelling

APPLICATION

Write the correct base word for each of the following "nonsense" words.

drelpy; topredy	drelpies _____	toprediest _____
gaty; chroty	gatious _____	chrotied _____

MINI-REVIEW!

Write the base word for each inflected "nonsense" word and write whether Inflectional Ending Generalization 1, 2, or 3 applies. The first one is done for you.

	Inflected Word	Base Word	Generalization Number
	habies	haby	3
tranlop; 2	tranlopping	_____	_____
sneby; 3	snebiest	_____	_____
clin; 2	clinning	_____	_____
frole; 1	froling	_____	_____
amsake; 1	amsaked	_____	_____
borsy; 3	borsiable	_____	_____

Syllabication

Introduction

Previously, we discovered that a vowel can generally be either a speech sound or an alphabetical letter (letters) representing that sound. But do vowels have any other significance?

Carefully pronounce these words then complete the blanks. The first one is done for you.

	Spelling	Dictionary Respelling	Number of Vowel Phonemes	Number of Syllables
	go	gō	1	1
2; 2	voodoo	voo′ doo	_____	_____
3; 3	minimize	mĭn′ ə mīz	_____	_____
4; 4	fraternity	frə tûr′ nĭ tē	_____	_____
5; 5	contradictory	kŏn′ trə dĭk′ tə rē	_____	_____
6; 6	nonparticipating	nŏn′ pär tĭs′ ə pā′ tĭng	_____	_____

syllables; sounds

We can conclude that a word contains the same number of [letters, syllables] as it has vowel [letters, sounds].

sound; letter

Therefore, each syllable contains one and only one vowel [letter, sound] and at least one vowel [letter, sound].

JUST FOR FUN!

1

a; I; e

u

How short can a syllable be? [1, 2, 3] letter as in the one-syllable words _____ and _____ or as in *evil* as represented by the letter _____ or in *tabular* as represented by the letter _____ .

How long can a syllable be? Five-letter words are fairly common as in *right* and _____ and six-letter ones can be found as in *throat, bright,* and _____. And there is even an eight-letter syllable that contains only one vowel letter. Hint: Sampson had it and it rhymes with *length*. It is _____.

wrong (or many other words)

strain, sprawl, scheme, etc.

strength

Syllabication Generalization: I

Are there visual or graphemic clues to dividing words into syllables?   Yes   No   And can we form generalizations that will allow us to syllabicate correctly an unrecognized word?   Yes   No

Yes

Yes

The first such generalization is so simple and obvious that you can state it immediately after examining the following words.

grape/vine	life/guard	whirl/wind
surf/board	snow/plow	stage/coach

A compound word is syllabicated between the two [syllables, words] comprising it.

words

Examine how the underlined words in each of these compound words is syllabicated.

but ter/fly   grass/hop per   blue/bon net

Are there visual and graphemic clues to this syllabication?

_____I doubt it.

_____Probably.

_____You bet there are!

You bet there are!

Syllabication Generalization: II

Why are these words from the previous lesson syllabicated where they are?

but ter   hop per   bon net

The spelling pattern *in the middle* of these words is commonly called the **?** pattern.

VCCV   _____VCCV   _____VCV   _____CVCV

Does this generalization also apply to VCCV words NOT containing *double* medial consonants? Examine these words.

tes <u>ti</u> fy   <u>ur</u> gent   <u>ig</u> nite   K<u>en</u> tuck y

GENERALIZE!

VCCV

consonant

When a word follows the [CVCV, VCCV] spelling pattern, to find syllables, divide between the two medial [vowel, consonant] letters.*

But why doesn't this principle work with these words?

1. so <u>pran</u> o   cy <u>cl</u>one   ni <u>tr</u>ate

2. a <u>chie</u>ve   mo<u>th</u> er   u<u>sh</u> er

blends

digraphs

In row 1 the underlined letters are consonant [blends, digraphs]. Those in row 2 are consonant [blends, digraphs].

Therefore, this generalization should be amended to state ". . . divide between the two medial consonant letters unless they represent a consonant

blend; digraph

_____ or a consonant _____."

APPLY!

Correctly syllabicate (/) these "nonsense" words.

kor/glop; cesh/er;
ab/bick; re/plact

k o r g o l p   c e s h e r   a b b i c k   r e p l a c t

Syllabication Generalization: III

Syllabicate these words according to the generalization you learned (hopefully) in the last lesson.

sid/le; og/le; lad/le

s i d l e   o g l e   l a d l e

---

*Written syllabication and pronunciation syllabication are not always identical. In writing, *mammal* is syllabicated *mam/mal*. But since the double *m*'s represent only one phoneme, in the pronunciation syllabication or a dictionary respelling, it is divided mam/al. This is true of most words containing double medial consonants.

closed	In this syllabication, the first syllable is [open, closed] and its vowel
short	phoneme would then be [long, short].

But here is the real syllabication of these words.

si/dle   o/gle   la/dle

open	Here, the first syllable is [open, closed] and its vowel phoneme is
long	[long, short].

If the "two consonant letters" generalization in the last lesson were followed with words such as these, the visual clue to the vowel sound

wrong	in the first syllable would be [wrong, right].

Therefore, we need another generalization.

last	When the [first, last] syllable of a word ends with the letters [le,
le; begins	el], the consonant letter preceding the *le* [begins, ends] the last syllable.*

Study these -*le* words.

strag′ gle   hum′ ble   dim′ ple

Yes	Do they follow the above generalization? Yes No

Therefore, this generalization also applies to words in which two consonant letters precede the -*le* ending.

However, in words containing a double medial consonant preceding the -*le* (*supple, quibble, haggle*), the written syllabication follows this generalization even though the second of the double consonant letters doesn't represent a phoneme (sup′ əl, kwib′ əl, hag′ əl).

APPLICATION!

Check and syllabicate (/) correctly any words below that follow these generalizations.

ga/ble; dwin/dle	_____g a b l e	_____d w i n d l e
bog/gle; am/ple	_____b o g g l e	_____a m p l e
cy/cle; bu/gle	_____c y c l e	_____b u g l e

---

*This principle is generally universally taught. However, the Ginn Reading 360, a major series of instructional materials, teaches children to syllabicate these words as follows: rumple—rump/le, gentle—gent/le.

Syllabication Generalization: IV

Notice the difference in how these two words are syllabicated.

<u>ro</u>bot—ro/bot   fr<u>ol</u>ic—frol/ic

VCV
after

For syllabication purposes, *the middle of* these words could be said to follow the [VCV, CVC] spelling pattern. Yet *robot* is syllabicated BEFORE the medial consonant while *frolic* is syllabicated _____ it.

The problem is that both patterns—V/CV and VC/V—occur with almost identical frequency!*

The best we can do is to teach children to try one way with an unrecognized word—and if they don't recognize the pronunciation, to try the other way! Rather than a generalization, we teach a strategy.

VCV
one
closed; liz/ard
short

A. If the first vowel letter in a [VCV, CVC] word is followed by just [one, two] consonant letter, first divide the word after the consonant to form a [open, closed] syllable as in [liz/ard, li/zard]. Give the first vowel letter the [long, short] vowel sound.

before; open
ti/ger; long

B. If you don't recognize the pronunciation of this word, divide it [before, after] the first consonant letter to form an [open, closed] syllable as in [ti/ger, tig/er]. Give the first vowel letter the [long, short] vowel sound.

Write A if these words follow the first step in this strategy, B if the second.

A; A; B
B; B; A

_____rivet   _____chili   _____Roman
_____finite   _____halo   _____damask

Syllabication Generalization: V

This last principle is so simple and easy to learn that we'll waste little time in getting to it. Visually study these words.

---

*See Appendix B for some sources listing the frequency with which these generalizations apply.

be/grudge   ex/hale   dis/prove   bi/sect   de/press

rest/less   tire/some   froth/y   graft/ing   prod/ded

If a word has an *affix* (prefix or suffix) and/or an inflectional ending,

affix   syllabicate between the base word and the _____ or between

ending   the base word and the inflectional _____.

Circle the word parts (prefix, suffix, or inflectional ending) in these words that form separate syllables.

(dis) tor (tion) ; jest (ing) (ly),

(trans) paren (cy); torren (tial)

(non) explo (sive) ; (un) avoid (a)(ble)

(pre) histor (ic) ; (re) adjust (ment)

distortion	jestingly
transparency	torrential
nonexplosive	unavoidable
prehistoric	readjustment

MINI-REVIEW

Correctly syllabicate the following words. Write whether Syllabication Generalization I, II, III, IV or V applies.

III, tri/fle; I, silk/worm

II, lar/va; IV, o/bese

II, a/pron; III, ea/gle

V, ail/ment; IV, mo/ment

IV, stat/ic; V and V,

un/beat/en

_____ t r i f l e	_____ s i l k w o r m
_____ l a r v a	_____ o b e s e
_____ a p r o n	_____ e a g l e
_____ a i l m e n t	_____ m o m e n t
_____ s t a t i c	_____ u n b e a t e n

Accenting

Introduction

We have repeatedly mentioned accented syllables in this book. But before we learn some principles governing this linguistic phenomenon, let's study accents for a minute.

Pronounce these common words naturally. Underline the syllable you believe is pronounced more forcefully and louder.*

level; baby; request;
explaining

accented

lev/el   ba/by   re/quest   ex/plain/ing

The syllable you underlined—and pronounced most forcefully—is the [accented, unaccented] syllable. It's as simple as that!

Or is it? Some multi-syllabic words have two accented syllables, one with the *primary* accent and another the *secondary* accent.

Circle the syllable with the primary accent and underline the one with the secondary accent. Caution: pronounce each word naturally.

satis(fac)tion; superin(ten)dent
in(vol)untary; demon(stra)tion

s a t i s f a c t i o n   s u p e r i n t e n d e n t

i n v o l u n t a r y   d e m o n s t r a t i o n

In this book we will deal *only* with the primary (or more forceful) accent and will use the primary accent mark (′) after the syllable to indicate the stressed syllable.

Accenting Generalization: I

Pronounce these words naturally. Underline the accented syllable in each one.

baseball; notebook; rainbow

vowel; phoneme; govern

Compound words:	base ball	note book	rain bow
Two-syllable words:	vow el	pho neme	gov ern

---

*A linguistic term commonly used to mean accent is *stress*. For our purposes, they are interchangeable synonyms.

Are you ready to form a generalization?

two · first — In compound and _____-syllable words, the accent is usually on the [first, second] word or syllable.

Does this apply to compound words in which the first word contains more than one syllable? Underline the accented syllable in these compound words.

bas; bod
dev; wa

bas ket ball	bod y guard
dev il fish	wa ter fall

first · first — In compound words in which the first word has more than one syllable, the accent probably falls on the [first, second] syllable of the [first, second] word.

But just to puzzle you (until the next page), circle the accented syllable in the following words, compare them with the above generalization.

rade; plain; lite

pa rade   com plain   po lite

first · second — In the above generalization, the [first, second] syllable was to be accented but in these words, the [first, second] syllable is accented.

Why? Are these exceptions? Or maybe they could be examples of another generalization?

Accenting Generalization: II

Is there a reason why *parade, complain,* and *polite* are NOT accented on the first syllable?

Compare the last syllable of the words in these columns.

am′ bush	a muse′
can′ cel	con ceal′
may′ or	ab stain′

glided — In column II, the vowel phoneme in the second syllable contains the [glided, unglided] sound.

And that leads us to the generalization.

two-
long or glided
accented

If the second syllable of a [one-, two-] syllable word contains a visual clue to a _____ vowel phoneme, then the second syllable is probably [accented, unaccented].

"QUICKIE" PRACTICE!
Check any words below that follow this generalization.

canteen; advice; congeal
evade

_____canteen _____advice _____congeal

_____evade _____pirate _____decade

Why don't *pirate* and *decade* follow this generalization? Are they examples of another generalization or merely exceptions to this one?

They're merely exceptions—as are *native, dandy, hormone, jumbo, hostile*—and numerous others. This generalization, like ALL the others we've studied can't be applied 100% of the time.* Nevertheless, it can be helpful to children learning to read.

Accenting Generalization: III

Study these words.
1. chaff′ <u>ing</u>   jilt′ <u>ed</u>
2. name′ <u>less</u>   glum′ <u>ly</u>   drunk′ <u>ard</u>   adapt′ <u>a ble</u>   joy′<u>ous</u>
3. <u>ab</u> nor′ mal   <u>be</u> friend′   <u>de</u> grade′   <u>ex</u> change′

base

The accented syllable in all these words is either the base word or part of the _____ word.

unaccented

And the underlined syllables are merely parts added to base words. These word parts are [accented, unaccented].

In row 1, the word parts are called inflectional endings.

suffixes

In row 2, they are [prefixes, suffixes].

prefixes

In row 3, they are [prefixes, suffixes].

Can you generalize an accenting principle using the above information?

---

*Remember Appendix B for sources giving the utility of these generalizations.

ending; prefix	If a word contains an inflectional _____, a _____,
suffix; base	or a _____, the accent falls on or within the _____ word.

Here is a list on some common affixes.*

Prefixes—a, ab, ad, an, be, con, com, col, de, dis, en, em, ex, in, im, il, ob, op, pre, pro, re, post, super, trans, sub, un

Suffixes—er, or, ist, ian, tion, sion, ry, ty, ity, al, able, ible, ment, ful, ic, ous, ious, ence, ance, ly, y

Accenting Generalization: IV

Accent (') the correct syllable in these words.

com′ pact; com pact′	That's her <u>com pact</u>. It will <u>com pact</u> the trash.
ob′ ject; ob ject′	What's that <u>ob ject</u>? Yes, I do <u>ob ject</u>!
No	Is *compact* accented the same in both sentences? Yes No
No	Is *object* accented the same in both sentences? Yes No

How can identically spelled words be accented differently?

In column I, the underlined words are what part of speech?

Nouns	Nouns Verbs Adjectives
first	And these words are accented on the f _ _ _ _ syllable.

In column II, the underlined words are what part of speech?

Verbs	Nouns Verbs Adjectives
second	And they are accented on the [first, second] syllable.

Complete this generalization.

	If a two-syllable word functions as both a noun and a verb, when
first	it is a noun, the accent is usually on the [first, second] syllable; when
second	it is a verb, the accent is usually on the [first, second] syllable.

Some words to which this generalization applies are: conduct, refuse, annex, discard, protest, affix, reject, convert, compress, record, escort, insert, incline, suspect, subject, and present.

---

*Because the meaning of affixes is beyond the scope of this book, only the printed affixes are given here. But reading programs typically teach the meanings of many of these.

After we teach children this phenomenon, we usually tell them, "If the first accent pattern you try doesn't sound natural, accent the other syllable and see if you recognize that word."

Review #6

1. Write the inflected form for each of these "nonsense" base words.

	Base Word		Inflectional Ending	Inflected Form
dapied	dapy	+	ed	_____
frebbing	freb	+	ing	_____
snurest	snure	+	est	_____
ambliddest	amblid	+	est	_____
woding	wode	+	ing	_____

2. A syllable must contain

_____A. at least one vowel sound.

A

_____B. at least one consonant sound.

3. Correctly syllabicate (/) these "nonsense" words.

caw/blop; er/chib

trans/rib/bing/ly; u/thone

or uth/one

brel/id or bre/lid; fa/cle

cawblop   erchib

transribbingly   uthone

brelid   facle

4. Accent (') the correct syllable in each of these "nonsense" words.

hand; sor

o; been

gret (if *un-* is a prefix); bosh

hand coat   sor kern

o ver light   ca been

un gret   bosh a ble

5. Write N if the underlined word is a noun, V if a verb. Then correctly accent (') these words.

V; pro test'

N; es' cort

N; con' vert

N; sub' ject

_____Will he pro test the decision?

_____Who is her es cort?

_____She's a con vert to Catholicism.

_____Phonics is my best sub ject.

6. Correctly syllabicate and accent these "nonsense" words.

| gom' melt; ab/tage' | g o m m e l t | a b t a g e |
| lesh' ious; sub/hist' ing | l e s h i o u s | s u b h i s t i n g |

SELF-EVALUATION #6

Total possible   26

My score   _____

I know it!	I'm learning it.	Phonics is my
_____I can apply it!	_____I try to apply it.	_____worst sub' ject!
		(or is it sub ject'?)

Putting It Altogether
(or The Last Roundup!)

Circle the correct answer. Some items may contain more than one correct answer.

Answers to this final review are on page 71.

1. The vowel phonemes are *a*, *e*, *i*, *o*, and *u*.   True   False
2. The breath channel is blocked or narrowed while producing consonants but not vowels.   True   False
3. How many phonemes in *marriage?*   2   3   4   5
4. A letter representing a phoneme is called a

    _____grapheme.

    _____pronunciation symbol.
5. In which "word" or "words" would the underlined letter (s) represent a glided vowel phoneme?

    str<u>o</u>nce   <u>o</u>p st   p<u>y</u>' trum   ca' t<u>i</u>ve   dr<u>o</u>ld
6. In which "word" would the underlined vowel letter(s) NOT represent a long vowel phoneme?

    bl<u>a</u>' fut   thr<u>u</u>te   fr<u>oa</u>m   spl<u>a</u>re   tr<u>i</u>ght

7. In which "word(s)" would the underlined letters represent a short vowel phoneme?

  scr<u>i</u>ld pl<u>i</u>dge <u>a</u> dote' <u>u</u>rnt <u>e</u>ltch

8. In which word(s) do(es) the underlined letter(s) represent the schwa phoneme?

  brid<u>a</u>l di<u>e</u>t ball<u>o</u>t capt<u>ai</u>n <u>a</u>bove

9. In which word(s) do the underlined letter(s) represent the circumflex *o* phoneme?

  w<u>o</u>rm p<u>ow</u>der f<u>au</u>lt ch<u>ai</u>r d<u>aw</u>n

10. In which "word(s)" would the underlined letters represent either of the two common vowel diphthongs?

  r<u>ou</u>th g<u>ui</u>nt sl<u>uy</u> fr<u>ow</u>l y<u>oi</u>ts

11. Which word(s) contain(s) the "short double *o*" phoneme?

  good blood door pool could

12. Which word(s) follow(s) the "vowel digraph" generalization?

  gr<u>ew</u> pl<u>ai</u>d br<u>ea</u>k c<u>oa</u>ch h<u>ea</u>rd

13. Which word(s) is/are NOT an exception to a common vowel phoneme-grapheme generalization?

  s<u>ou</u>l t<u>o</u> h<u>au</u>nt g<u>e</u>t br<u>oa</u>d

14. Which word does NOT contain one or more letters that do not represent phonemes ("silent" letters)?

  cello listen might church chalk

15. Which of these letter groups represents the four most common consonant digraphs?

  th cr spr wh sc fl ch sh br

16. In which word(s) do(es) the *th* represent the voiced phoneme (ŦH)?

  <u>th</u>ere <u>th</u>orn ba<u>th</u> fai<u>th</u> mo<u>th</u>er

17. In which "word(s)" would the underlined letter represent a "hard" phoneme?

  to<u>c</u> prea<u>c</u>din <u>c</u>lett dor<u>g</u>ud abo<u>g</u>e

18. A syllable is—

_____ A. two or more letters with one sound.

_____ B. the smallest possible speech sound.

_____ C. adjacent vowel and consonant sounds.

_____ D. a speech unit with one vowel sound.

19. What is the base word for the inflected "word" *drudding?*

                drud   drude   drudd   drudde

20. Which word(s) is/are syllabicated wrongly?

        lad y   ab rupt   peop le   bac on   pho nics

21. Which is the correct syllabication for *budable?*

         bu da ble   bud a ble   bud ab le   bu dab le

22. Which "word(s)" is/are accented correctly?

       tur kune′   pha′ net   eeb ing′   ol′ tush   note ball′

23. Which "word" is syllabicated and accented wrongly?

    lup′ i cap ping   let ha′ ble   gro mike′ ly   am bil′ i ty

24. Which is the correct syllabication and accenting for *undrethonting?*

         un dre thont′ ing   und reth′ ont ing

         undre′ thont ing   un dret′ hon ting

25. In which sentence is the underlined word accented correctly?

_____ A. The <u>af fix′</u> changed the meaning of the word.

_____ B. Wool fibers <u>con′ tract</u> in hot water.

_____ C. Don't <u>pro′ test</u> the decision.

_____ D. <u>Dis card′</u> all the torn pages.

ANSWERS

1. False
2. True
3. 5
4. grapheme
5. p_y' trum; dr_o_ld
6. spl_a_re
7. pl_i_dge; _e_ltch
8. brid_a_l; di_e_t; ball_o_t; captain; _a_bove
9. f_au_lt; d_aw_n
10. r_ou_th; fr_ow_l; y_oi_ts
11. good; could
12. c_oa_ch
13. h_au_nt; get
14. church
15. th; wh; ch; sh
16. _th_ere; mo_th_er
17. to_c_; preac_d_in; _c_lett; dor_g_ud
18. D
19. drud
20. lad y; ab rupt; peop le; bac on; pho nics
21. bud a ble
22. tur kune'; pha' net; ol' tush
23. let ha' ble
24. un dre thont' ing
25. D

DID I PUT IT ALL TOGETHER?

_____Yes!   _____Probably   _____Back to the ol' drawing board!

Appendix A
Major Decoding Generalizations
in This Book

Vowels and Consonants

1. A vowel sound is a sound in which the breath channel is not blocked or narrowed during production.
2. A consonant sound is a sound in which the breath channel is blocked or narrowed during production.

Phonemes and Graphemes

1. A phoneme is the smallest unit of sound that distinguishes one word from another.
2. A grapheme is an alphabetical letter or cluster of letters representing a phoneme.

Vowel Phonemes

1. Long or glided vowel phonemes "say the name" of the alphabet letter representing that sound. These phonemes are represented by pronunciations topped by a macron: $\bar{a}$, $\bar{e}$, $\bar{\imath}$, $\bar{o}$, $\bar{u}$.
2. Short or unglided vowel phonemes are heard at the beginning of *at, Ed, if, ox,* and *up.* These phonemes are frequently represented by pronunciation symbols topped by a breve: $\breve{a}$, $\breve{e}$, $\breve{\imath}$, $\breve{o}$, $\breve{u}$.
3. The *r*-controlled vowel phonemes are neither glided nor unglided. The phoneme /r/ affects the pronunciation of vowel phonemes immediately preceding it in a syllable, e.g., *car, for, her, care,* etc. The four commonest *r*-controlled phonemes are frequently represented by the pronunciation symbols *är* as in *car,* *ôr* as in *for,* *ûr* as in *her,* and *ãr* as in *care.*
4. The circumflex *o* phoneme is heard at the beginning of *all* and *awe.* It is represented by the pronunciation symbol *ô.*

5. Vowel diphthongs are two vowel phonemes continuously glided or blended together within the same syllable. The two major ones are heard at the beginning of *ouch* and *oil*. These are represented by the pronunciation symbols *ou* and *oi*.

6. The short double *o* phoneme is heard in the words *wood* and *foot*. It is represented by the pronunciation symbol o͞o (u̇).

7. The long double *o* phoneme is heard in the words *food* and *pool*. It is represented by the pronunciation symbol o͞o (ü).

8. The schwa phoneme is heard at the beginning of the words *above* and *occur*. It is represented by the pronunciation symbol ə.

Vowel Phoneme-Grapheme Generalizations

1. When a one-syllable word or a final accented syllable ends in the VCe spelling pattern, the vowel letter usually represents the glided vowel phoneme and the final *e* does not represent a sound.

2. In most VCe words with the vowel letter *u*, the *u* may represent the long *u* sound as in *cute* and *fuse* or the long double *o* sound as in *rule* and *flute*.

3. In many VCe words in which *r* is the consonant letter, the preceding vowel letter may not represent its glided vowel phoneme. The *r* affects the preceding vowel phoneme, giving it one of several unique *r*-controlled sounds.

4. When one of the vowel digraphs, *ai*, *ay*, *ea*, *ee*, or *oa*, is in the middle of a one-syllable word or an accented syllable, the vowel digraph represents a glided or long vowel phoneme.

5. If a one-syllable word or an accented syllable contains only one vowel letter and that vowel letter is at the end of the word or syllable, that letter usually represents its long or glided vowel phoneme.

6. The vowel letter in the graphemic bases -*ight*, -*ind*, and -*old* represents its glided or long vowel phoneme.

7. When a single vowel letter is in a CVC spelling pattern, either in a one-syllable word or an accented syllable, that letter usually represents its unglided or short vowel phoneme.

8. When a single vowel letter is the first letter in a closed syllable, either in a one-syllable word or an accented syllable, that letter usually represents its unglided or short vowel phoneme.

9. When the letter *a* is immediately followed by a *u* or a *w*, either in a one-syllable word or an accented syllable, that letter usually represents the circumflex *o* phoneme.

10. The graphemes *ou* and *ow* usually represent the vowel diphthong /aw/ which is represented by the pronunciation symbol *ou*.

11. The graphemes *oi* and *oy* usually represent the vowel diphthong /ɔy/ which is represented by the pronunciation symbol *oi*.

12. If a one-syllable word or an accented syllable contains the *oo* grapheme, try the "long double *o* phoneme" as in *pool* and *room.* If you don't recognize this pronunciation, try the "short double *o* phoneme" as in *stood* and *hook.*

13. A vowel letter or cluster in an unaccented syllable usually represents the schwa phoneme, /ə/.

Consonant Phonemes

1. The phonemes represented by consonant graphemes blend almost inseparably with the vowel or consonant phonemes following them, making it difficult if not impossible to isolate them for pronunciation purposes.

2. A consonant blend, or cluster, is two- or three-consonant letters that represent more than one consonant phoneme blended together so smoothly as to be virtually inseparable, e.g., <u>bl</u>end, <u>fr</u>oze, <u>sm</u>oke, and <u>thr</u>ew.

3. A consonant digraph is two consonant letters representing one consonant phoneme. The most common are the four represented by *ch*, *sh*, *th*, and *wh* respectively in the words *chip, ship, them (think),* and *whip*.

4. The consonant digraph *th* represents two common phonemes, the voiced as in *there* and *that,* and the unvoiced as in *thin* and *thank*.

5. In some consonant letter clusters, only one letter represents a phoneme as in <u>w</u>rite, <u>kn</u>ife, and la<u>mb</u>.

Consonant Phoneme-Grapheme Generalizations

1. The following 17 single consonant letters are phonetically consistent. Whenever they represent a consonant phoneme by themselves and not in conjunction with other consonant letters, they usually represent the same consonant phoneme: *b, d, f, h, j, k, l, m, n, p, q, r, t, v, w, y, z.*

2. When the grapheme *c* is followed by the letter *e*, or *i*, or *y*, it usually represents the *soft c* phoneme /s/ as in the words *cent, city,* and *cymbals.*

3. When the grapheme *c* is followed by any letter other than *e* or *i* or *y*, or when it is the last letter in a word or syllable, it usually represents the /k/ phoneme and is frequently called the *hard c* sound.

4. When the grapheme *g* is followed by the letter *e* or *i* or *y*, it usually represents the *soft g* phoneme /j/ as in the words *gentle, giant,* and *gypsy.*

5. When the grapheme *g* is followed by any letter other than *e* or *i* or *y*, or when it is the last letter in a word or syllable, it usually represents the *hard g* phoneme.

6. In a doubled consonant grapheme, the two letters usually represent a single consonant sound.

Inflectional Ending Generalizations

1. When a base word ends in "final *e*," drop the *e* before adding an inflectional ending beginning with a vowel letter.
2. When the last three letters of a base word end with the CVC spelling pattern, double the final consonant letter before adding an inflectional ending (or a suffix) beginning with a vowel letter.
3. When a base word ends with the letter *y* preceded by a consonant letter, change the *y* to *i* before adding an inflectional ending (or a suffix) beginning with a vowel letter—other than *-ing*.

Syllabication Generalizations

1. Each syllable contains one and only one vowel sound and at least one vowel letter.
2. A compound word is syllabicated between the two words comprising it. Then divide the words that form the compound following the generalizations presented.
3. When a word follows the VCCV spelling pattern, to find syllables, divide between the two medial consonant letters unless they represent a consonant blend or a consonant digraph.
4. When the last syllable of a word ends with the letters *le*, the consonant letter preceding the *le* begins the last syllable. This generalization also applies to words in which two consonant letters precede the *-le* ending.
5. If the first vowel letter in a VCV word is followed by a single consonant letter, first divide the word *after* the consonant to form a closed syllable as in *liz ard*. Give the first vowel letter the short vowel sound.
6. If you don't recognize the pronunciation of the word obtained from the application of the above principle, divide the word *before* the

first consonant letter to form an open syllable as in *ti ger*. Give the first vowel letter the long vowel sound.

7. If a word has an affix (prefix or suffix) and/or an inflectional ending, syllabicate between the base word and the affix or between the base word and the inflectional ending.

Accenting Generalizations

1. In compound and two-syllable words, the accent is usually on the first word or syllable.

2. In compound words in which the first word has more than one syllable, the accent probably falls on the first syllable of the first word.

3. If the second syllable of a two-syllable word contains a visual clue to a long vowel phoneme, then the second syllable is probably accented.

4. If a word contains an inflectional ending, a prefix, or a suffix, the accent falls on or within the base word.

5. If a two-syllable word functions as both a noun and a verb, when it is a noun, the accent is usually on the first syllable; when it is a verb, the accent is usually on the second syllable.

Appendix B
Sources on the Utility of Decoding Generalizations

Bailey, Mildred Hart, "The Utility of Phonic Generalizations in Grades One Through Six," *The Reading Teacher*, 22 (February 1967), 413–418.

Burmeister, Lou E., "Usefulness of Phonic Generalizations," *The Reading Teacher*, 21 (January 1968), 349–356, 360.

Burmeister, Lou E., "Vowel Pairs," *The Reading Teacher*, 21 (February 1968), 445–452.

Burmeister, Lou E., "Final Vowel-Consonant-e," *The Reading Teacher*, (February 1971), 439–442.

Burrows, Alvina Treut and Zyra Lourie, "When 'Two Vowels Go Walking,'" *The Reading Teacher*, (November 1963), 79–82.

Clymer, Theodore, "The Utility of Phonic Generalizations in the Primary Grades," *The Reading Teacher*, 16 (January 1963), 252–258.

Emans, Robert, "The Usefulness of Phonic Generalizations Above the Primary Grades," *The Reading Teacher*, 22 (February 1967), 419–425.

Harris, Albert J. and Edward R. Sipay, *Effective Teaching of Reading*, 2nd edition, David McKay Co., Inc., New York, 1971, 247–251.

Oaks, Ruth E., "A Study of the Vowel Situations in a Primary Vocabulary," *Education*, (May 1952), 604–617.

Spache, George D. and Evelyn B. Spache, *Reading in the Elementary School*, 3rd edition, Allyn and Bacon, Inc., Boston, 1973, 462–470.

Winkley, Carol, "Which Accent Generalizations Are Worth Teaching?" *The Reading Teacher*, 20 (December 1966), 219–224.

PRINTED IN U.S.A.